VOICEPRINT:

How to find your voice, live your song, and unleash your purpose.

LONNA HARDIN

ISBN: 978-0-9996630-7-3

To my parents, Shirley Jean Clark and the Reverend Eugene E. Hardin, "May your life, legacy and memory be forever blessed. Thank you for giving me the seeds to cultivate my voiceprint. Your life, love, and leadership still inspire me and make me want to be a better woman."

To my own daughter Mya Love Boyd who echoes my own voiceprint but will reverberate much louder and more powerfully through the universe, "May your voiceprint open doors, opportunities and only take you on a path to give you happiness, blessings and fulfill your highest dreams. You are the best part of me, my 2.0 and 3.0."

To Margi, Vanessa, Renata, and Brenda, "Thanks for being the best sisters a girl could ask for." To my brothers Eugene Jr. and Xavier, big sis loves you! Finally, to my nieces, nephews, godchildren, and extended family near and far, always remember: "The only way to right history is to write history!" It's time to unleash your voiceprint!

To my parents, Shirley Jean Clark and the Reverend Eugene E. Hardin, "May your life, legacy and memory be forever blessed. Thank you for giving me the seeds to cultivate my voiceprint. Your life, love, and leadership still inspire me and make me want to be a better woman."

To my own daughter Mya Love Boyd who echoes my own voiceprint but will reverberate much louder and more powerfully through the universe, "May your voiceprint open doors, opportunities and only take you on a path to give you happiness, blessings and fulfill your highest dreams. You are the best part of me, my 2.0 and 3.0."

To Margi, Vanessa, Renata, and Brenda, "Thanks for being the best sisters a girl could ask for." To my brothers Eugene Jr. and Xavier, big sis loves you! Finally, to my nieces, nephews, godchildren, and extended family near and far, always remember: "The only way to right history is to write history!" It's time to unleash your voiceprint!

Contents

Contents

CHAPTER 1

Microphone Check

Ever been shopping? Suddenly you stop. You think you hear a familiar voice. Or watch a television commercial? Suddenly getting overwhelmed by the "guess who it is" syndrome? You recognize the voice on screen. Maybe your phone rings. Before you ask who, it is, the person says, "Hello?" You immediately know it's your loved one or long-time friend.

The human voice is so unique, powerful, and full of command. It mesmerizes, captivates, and penetrates. It leaves an impression on the ear and heart.

For example, the mother who hears the cry of her newborn baby. Instantly, she stops what she's doing to find what's wrong. Without being taught, the baby instinctively knows the power of using its voice. The baby recognizes, if asserted with proper emotion, its mother will come. The baby doesn't need to be taught what I'm going to teach you. It immediately knows its power and ability without being told. It doesn't doubt itself or ask questions like:

"Where do I come from?"
"How much money do I have in the bank?"
"Will people believe in me?"
"Can I really do it?"
"Will I fail, or will I succeed?"

In that moment the baby wants something more than to continue in discomfort. It wants its mother, "Now!"

Maybe you're like that newborn baby. You're experiencing pain or discomfort in your life. You're unsure of how to make it go away. This is the moment. Stop. Put down the book. Open your mouth and scream. Help is on the way!

Every human being is a distinct voice. We're each are born with the intrinsic gift to leave our impression on the world. This voice can be used to change the world or incite hate. It can speak life and love into everyone you meet.

Or, it can be used to criticize, belittle and tear down. It can change environments, alter the course of a nation, and affect generations. It can galvanize, bring together, and propel forward. But, if not properly channeled, it can also divide, alienate, and hold back.

Just like a thumbprint used to identify someone's identity, or a blueprint used to design and construct a building, so is the ability to be identified by the sound your inward being emanates, carries, and projects.

It's your voiceprint. It's much more powerful, valuable, and significant than you can imagine. It's like a voice or song. Once entered another person's soul or hearing, it never leaves. If powerful enough, it gets stuck in their head. Like a beautiful melody, it comes back at the most unexpected times to replay over and over again.

Your distinct voiceprint can carry you places never dreamed. Or if uncultivated, keep you locked in a pattern of destructive habits never to be escaped.

Here's what's beautiful. We all have one. We're each gifted with the ability to influence or make a lasting impression. We can contribute something so significant it draws people, places, and things into our lives to influence and affect others.

Your voiceprint can attract anything you need.

Your voiceprint is who you are. It's what you bring to the table. It's all you have to offer and give. It's you at your core. It's you at your best.

We each have the ability to tap into our voiceprint. If you're reading this book, you're destined to tap into your highest potential and "Live Your Song." Unfortunately, what I find in my travels is many don't know exactly what I mean when I say, "Live Your Song." Some think it means to go find your favorite song to loudly start blasting it through your car audio!

"Living Your Song" is about being true to who you are.

It's to understand how your experiences in life make you the person you are. Each experience can be used to change the world.

It's about legacy, taking your life to the top of the charts and staying there. It's about carefully crafting the highs and lows of life, weaving the pauses and rests; Orchestrating the sharps and flats into a beautiful anthem that forever resonates in the universe.

The more I speak to everyday people, old and young, I realize most aren't even close to living their song. Many don't have a clue what their song is. They don't know what they stand for or believe. Some are still unsure of who they really are. Others still struggle to find their voice.

Need proof? Look at the Kardashian wannabes or those who proclaim to "All Hail the Queen." They become Beyoncé copycats. Or what about the Rhianna impersonators of the world? It's easier to sit in the audience at a concert and cheer for someone else. Or go to the store to finance someone else's product, brand or dream.

What about stopping to take the time to claim, own, and build your own?

This doesn't apply to everyone. Some truly like good music and beautiful talent. Most, on the other hand, refuse to go through the process to discover their own voiceprint. Many are lost living "someone else's song." They'd rather turn on the television to be entertained or tune in to the radio to drown out the pain their own life brings.

For example, I get exacerbated with social media. Scrolling through time lines listening to videos or reading posts. Everyone's a "Boss." Constantly bombarded with photos of social media celebrities, alleged success gurus, and the next millennial influencer. In my experience I find everyone wants to look the part, but few want to do the work needed to actually "be" the part.

I'm not talking about the success of being a fitness guru, the next big life coach, or Instagram page with 1,000,000 followers. I mean the work of finding your voice, what you bring to the table and determining your voiceprint.

How will your life leave someone else's life better? How will you leave the world in a better place?

When you take your last breath, what will your voiceprint say?

Will you be like everyone else? Those looking to Hollywood, Netflix, YouTube, Google and the movie screen to find what's trending next. Those who can't wait to hop on board? Others go hard at seeking to be relevant losing true relevance in the process.

Hollywood makes billions selling images, songs, movies, and false realities to everyday people. So many long to escape their own true reality. Many want prestige, fortune, glamour, and the spotlight television bring.

What about the hard work, discipline, suffering, isolation and seclusion?

If everyone would take time to truly discover the power of their own voiceprint, Hollywood would become obsolete. Tourists would no longer travel to the historic entertainment industry hub to take pictures of celebrity footprints of on a small sidewalk strip.

By the way, what is a star anyway? By definition, a star is "A fixed luminous point in the night sky that is a large, remote incandescent body like the sun." More importantly, "it is a luminous ball of gas *held together by its own gravity.*"

Why do we look outside of ourselves for the power we already possess? Everything we need is within.

Hollywood learned this secret long ago. They learned to make money highlighting the exceptional gifts, work ethic and talents of others.

Ever wondered why celebrities get paid millions to endorse a product, appear in a commercial, star in a movie or record a voiceover for a radio spot? Each celebrity possesses something distinctly setting them apart from others auditioning for the role.

It's their stunning looks or compelling charm. The person draws the attention of hundreds of thousands. People pay to attend their concert or see them perform. Is it just because he or she is an amazing entertainer and gives a good show?

Earlier this year, I went to visit my mother. She was watching a Lifetime movie. I don't often spend much time watching TV. Within two to three minutes of arriving, my focus immediately shifted to the screen.

I heard a familiar voice. I looked up to find it was well-known celebrity, former rapper, and talk show host, Queen Latifah. I observed her body movements, face expressions, and story line delivery. Was it her moving words?

No. I recognized the "voiceprint?"

Movie execs, casting agents, record labels, and music producers each share the secret. If you can find the right voiceprint, you bring home the Oscar, win the Grammy, and top sales charts. Powerful, distinct voiceprints gain the affection of loyal fans who'll come back again and again.

You are the voice... the star waiting to make your entrance. "Will you show up?" "Will you appear?"

It's your time to shine. You don't have to live like most who spend their lives wasting their voiceprint on people who can't appreciate it or benefit from its power. No more waiting in the shadows!

The time is now for you to take center stage and listen to the song within. Your voice was created to share with the world.

This book is for you if:

- ✓ You are starting completely over after experiencing a roadblock or setback
- ✓ You lost your motivation and don't know how to get it back
- ✓ You are stuck in a dead-end job or career
- ✓ You are a high school or college dropout
- ✓ You feel like your life is meaningless and you have no sense of purpose
- ✓ You are tired of following the crowd and living status quo
- ✓ You are a first time single parent raising a child alone
- ✓ You grew up in a single parent household with little family support

- ✓ You are in a toxic relationship and don't know how to get out

Even if blindsided by life stop licking your wounds, you can recover!

The first step forward before you find your voiceprint, is to "Live Your Song." Sing it to everyone you meet. Understand, appreciate, and realize the power you have been given.

There's something unique about you. The sum of your experiences in life – both good and bad – contribute to the person you see in the mirror each day. Add your talents, gift, and the wealth of knowledge you gained on your journey. There's no one else like you and never will be!

You have something valuable to share with the world. It's the impression you leave with the lives you touch and everyone you meet – your unique voiceprint. Some of us go through life never realizing we're unique and wonderfully made. Many get up each day, get ready for work, get our kids ready for school, drive to work, put in 8 hours a day, come home, cook, put our kids to bed, sleep, and wake up the next day to do it all again.

- ✓ *Are you just going through the motions?*
- ✓ *Do you live a life that allows you to share your voice with the world?*
- ✓ *As a teenager did you have all these dreams about changing the world? What happened?*
- ✓ *Did you finish college and went straight to work so that you could pay off your student loans?*

- ✓ *Did you meet a great guy, get married, and somehow forget the sound of your own voice?*
- ✓ *Do you have kids and figure all those "crazy" ideas are best left in the past?*

Have you lost your song and wonder where your "true" voice has gone? Sadly, many are singing "the blues" never regaining their voice. And then, there are those who die and go to their graves never having shared or released it.

You have the opportunity to use your unique voiceprint to make a lasting impact. You can leave behind a legacy, not just for your children but the world. There is value in your voice. When activated it creates and leaves behind to impression that can influence a generation, community, nation, and world.

Why is it important to know your voiceprint?

No matter where I go, I always share, *"The only way to "right" history is to "write history"*. Do you want to determine your own history and leave a legacy to impact those around you and the world?

Find your unique voiceprint. Tell your story. Release the power and authenticity of your own "true" voice.

Without a voiceprint, you will drift through life stuck.

Are you thinking:

I am tired of the same old, same old!
I have more to offer!
I have no purpose to life!

Am I just living to die?
Life is too hard!
Whatever... It is what it is!
Why do I even try?
Things will never change!

Once you activate your voiceprint, your mindset changes and your voice sounds like:

I have the power to make a difference!
I create the best version of myself every day!
Yes! I live a life "in purpose on purpose."
I am a living legacy!
When I activate my voice, life is so much easier!
I make choices now that determine my future!
I activate and affect change with my voice!
I have the power to change!

The process starts now. Get still. Embrace the silence. Hear the voice within. Once set free it can't be silenced. It's ready to be unlocked and unleashed to make its lasting impression on the world.

Take out a paper and pen. Write three action steps you can begin doing today to start listening to your own unique voice. Make each as specific as you can. Reflect on ways you will hold yourself accountable. Set aside 15 minutes a day to journal your thoughts.

ACTION STEPS

1) ____

2) ____

3) ____

CHAPTER 2

Why Now?

Imagine a child born without a voice. They've lost the ability to cry when something is wrong. They're unable to communicate if happy or sad. As they grow, there's no ability to call to mom or dad when needed. Voice gives expression. Without voice, there are less clues to tell when someone's entered the room. Voice gives us the power to articulate words and interpret meaning.

I struggled with my own voice. I'd find myself in an intense meeting knowing I had the answer everyone was looking for. Often sitting, waiting for a chance to chime in, someone with a stronger personality or voice interrupted unapologetically. These voices took over to dominate the conversation. It went an entirely different direction with little resolution.

Holding back became a pattern. I withheld true thoughts, ideals and beliefs. Sometimes, because I needed the approval of others. Others, because I lacked the energy and stamina to argue my point.

Social media has increased a new online trend. I call it "Personal voice dominance." This trend has taken online conversations to a new level.

Do you remember the 2016 Presidential election? If you read online news, followed Twitter or kept up with candidate debates, you saw it. People were voicing their opinions at an alarming rate. Some without any regard for others.

Discussions around race, politics, money, and business became so tense and heightened. Often, it was like being in an online boxing match. What we found whether online or a tv debate is the loudest, strongest, most perceived powerful voice won. Whether by rhetoric, wealth, media or political affiliation, the loudest voice possessed the power to sway the masses, influence public opinion and change polls.

Unfortunately, after election polls closed and the final candidate announced, there was a swift reality that kicked in. It became more and more evident that some voices in the debate weren't representative of real people with real opinions. They were bots joining the conversation when important dialogue was needed the most.

These artificial voices favorably tipped the results in the direction they wanted the conversation to go. They infiltrated the system giving credibility to those who would otherwise have none.

Can you relate? Just when at a crucial time in our lives or a crossroads ready to stand up for what we believe, some voice infiltrates the conversation.

For some, it's the voice of fear. For others, it's the voice of doubt. Some struggle to silence the voice of shame.

If you're like me, it's a mix. These voices compete for the chance to have the final say. They strive for the chance to chime in on the direction you're headed. So many campaigning to convince you they should take the lead.

When I first set out to write this book it was simply to heal and uncover some of the childhood trauma I repressed, forgot and locked away. *I needed answers.* I had questions about why my life had taken a certain path. I also had questions about why all roads led me further away from the person I loved and longed to be.

As a children's book author and out-of-school time enrichment provider, I attend meetings, conferences and professional development trainings in the youth development space. Informed trauma care is a very hot topic right now. Organizations are beginning to understand it's virtually impossible to reach and teach people traumatized by life events.

Those impacted get stuck unable to move forward. This new psychological approach is a huge win for those suffering in silence in need of unconventional intervention. But what does a person who grew up prior to this do?

What does a person do who's carried the pain for years, sometimes decades? What about those who had to bare the shame for years? They've lived with the torment not telling a soul about the trauma they've faced.

I started writing this book as a reminder of all I'd overcome. I needed to pull back the layers and celebrate the many times I'd persevered. I needed to give myself the chance to look back. I had never taken time to reflect on what made my own song so powerful. I was more than a beautiful face and voice behind a microphone. What made my personal song so distinct was what I had fought through.

No one but God knew the internal voices I had to block out of my mind. Every time I sang I had to fight through the noise to release the sounds and melodies hidden in my heart. I carried shame from buried traumatic childhood and teenage memories. Singing and music was my escape.

As I built the confidence to truly open and up and be transparent about these events, I realized this book was not about me at all.

Countless other individuals also endured the excruciating process of suffering in silence with no one to come to their aid. A lawyer argues a court case. An attorney is assigned to both the defendant and plaintiff. This allows the judge to hear both sides of the story. Once the entire story is heard, the jury brings the final verdict, so justice can be served.

What about those like me whose case was never heard? Those whose day in court never came. They have no defense. No one's heard their story. There was no voice of affirmation letting them know someone recognized and heard their pain.

My focus shifted. I wept for the voiceless who live with their shame and suffer daily. They don't know they have the power to change the course of their life. No one argued their case.

The book transformed from a personal tell all to a purpose driven tool to help unlock and unleash others. Some personal experiences are far too complex to briefly share in the pages of this book. I do share more when speaking to audiences in safe spaces.

Many I speak with are also survivors of traumatic events. Their lives have been altered. They rarely have trusted spaces where they can safely heal. We all need affirming, reassuring voices that allow us to be vulnerable. They just listen. They understand and listen from a place of authenticity, sensitivity, connectivity and compassion.

Through my love and passion for music, I began to understand why a voice can transform meaningless, empty words into a beautiful anthem. I started to understand the power a voice holds to heal.

Everyone has certain qualities hidden in their voice. You can hear it whether in a tiny infant, nagging mom, overprotective dad, aging parent, angry child, or stern teacher. Regardless of race, color, gender or religion, each voice has a distinct, lasting sound.

Within the sound is a vibration. Some vibrations are inviting and welcoming. Others are peaceful and serene. While others make you cringe and want to run away. This is a simple way to understand the dynamics that operate behind our own unique voiceprint.

A voiceprint is much more significant than just a voice alone.

It's who we are and what we're made of. It's the vibe we carry inside. It's the sound we omit to the universe. It's the way we interact with the world. It's how we impact others. It's the impression we leave in those around us and the world.

Our voiceprint is the frequency we operate and live from.

Once a life is impacted by a voiceprint, it can't shake it. It enlightens and inspires. It brings that life into alignment causing it to reflect on a time, event, moment, or possibility. A voiceprint transforms a nation, shifts a course of action, or invokes change.

Some of the world's most powerful, transformative history makers were able to find and recognize the value of their voiceprint at an early age.

People like:

Jesus Christ proclaiming himself to be the Son of God.

Nelson Mandela who spent years incarcerated unjustly standing for what he believed breaking the noose of apartheid from off his people.

Ghandi who took on the burden of a nation and cause of an oppressed people.

Mother Teresa who was more concerned about the poor than titles and possessions.

Harriet Tubman born into slavery but after experiencing freedom risking her own life to help others.

Frederick Douglass who used his writings and voice to take on the Goliath of slavery.

Sojourner Truth an abolitionist who took on racism and feminism when unpopular and "she too" was not even a thought in existence.

George Carver Washington Jr. a revolutionary inventor who changed the game of economics using a peanut.

Reverend Martin Luther King Jr. whose prophetic vision and voice altered the course of history for black Americans across the U.S. shaking the oppressive hand of economic disparities and injustice.

Emperor Haile Selassie who led the resistance to the Italian invasion of Ethiopia and modernized his country.

Princess Diana who walked as royalty known as the "People's Princess. Her life's work was to help those suffering with HIV Aids.

There are so many more to name: Bob Marley, Michael Jackson, Whitney Houston, President Barack Obama, First Lady Michelle Obama, Steve Jobs, Oprah Winfrey, Derek Jeter, John Legend and the list goes on.

Each have powerful stories of having an "Aha" moment where they recognized and understood their voiceprint. They made a decision to lift their vibration to the universe and make sure everyone was listening to take note.

They each had core common beliefs:

- The power of their voice was in their own hands.
- They had an authentic story to share and give.
- They could leave an impact to make a difference.

- They needed to be resilient and put action to their faith.
- Intellectual property and what you contribute to the world is more valuable than money, status, cars, and things.
- Sweat equity earned through experiences, struggle and suffering will always pay dividends.

As a result, these world changers have gone down in history leaving their mark on the world. They give us a glimpse into what can happen when we gain clarity about who we are and discover our own voiceprint. We can then leave a mark on humanity that says, "I was here."

Finding your voiceprint is not about clinging to your successes and victories. It's not about shunning the dark, hidden parts of your identity. In contrast, it's facing your fears. It's admitting your shame. More than anything, it's making a conscious decision that the parts of you that deserve to be exclaimed will.

When you have the power and audacity to own your voiceprint, you will unleash a power inside that can't be stopped. It can't be contained or controlled. It opens doors allowing you to elevate to places in time to reconstruct your past and redefine your future.

There's one formula I've created and learned to live by. Each of the game changers above tapped into it long before I was born. I'll touch on it much more later in the book. If you get this concept, it will change your life. It is:

VOICE + VISION = VELOCITY

When you unleash the power of your voiceprint, your life will begin to move ahead full speed. Later, we'll also go into more detail about two major laws that govern the universe and why this is.

For now, it's important to note that when our words and actions line up with who we say we are and who we say we want to be, **"shift happens."** That's right, "shift."

We began to shift our perspectives. We shift our families. We shift our businesses. We shift our relationships. We shift our finances. We shift our futures. We elevate and begin to shift our lives into the realities we've always dreamed.

This shift causes elevation.

The more we shift the more we elevate, the more we leave behind frequencies, mindsets, behaviors, patterns and toxic relationships that no longer serve our voiceprint.

Since really getting clear about the enormous totality of what we carry and have to offer can be daunting, I created a free tool to help you through the process called the Voice Map Canvas. We'll provide more information on this later too.

In the canvas, we review authentic voice, vision, and strategies to begin identifying your unique voiceprint.

In 2015 I graduated with my Master of Science in Internet Marketing from Full Sail University.

I went back to school as an Entrepreneur determined to take back the power of my own voiceprint. I wanted to stop being dependent on others to bring the vision I had in my heart to help voiceless people, single mothers, and children of single parents to reality.

Ironically, wanting to help give voice to others helped me persevere through working two full time jobs, a part -time job, caring for my mother, and raising a daughter as a single mother alone. I was determined to provide a life for others I desperately wanted to experience but failed.

Digital marketing taught me a lot. It stretched my thinking. I met amazing people, learned new skills, and grew. In marketing, you often hear about the 7 P's of marketing. When designing a voice map to help people discover their highest potential, I also created 7 key P discovery areas hidden inside an unlocked voiceprint.

Each when identified will help propel you into your future. We'll dig deeper into this later, but let's quickly review them here. The 7 key discovery areas on the journey to unleashing your voiceprint are:

1. **PURPOSE**
2. **PASSION**
3. **POWER**
4. **PRINCIPLE**
5. **POSITIONING**
6. **PRACTICE**
7. **PROJECT**

Taking time to really get clear about your existence and what makes you unique is critical. In the Voice Map Canvas, we walk you through additional exercises and reflections.

Understanding these 7 defining elements is key. A person who takes the time to dig deep inside to uncover the value of who they are and the power they carry inside will impact others in profound ways. Are you ready to discover, unlock, and unleash your voiceprint?

Make a list of the top five characteristics hidden in your voiceprint.

These can be qualities others have complimented you on or unique qualities you've never shared. Take time to really think each one through before adding it to your list. Make sure each resonate with who you really are.

1) ______________________________

2) ______________________________

3) ______________________________

4) ______________________________

5) ______________________________

CHAPTER 3

My Voiceprint

Even as a child, I couldn't escape my voiceprint. I have always loved people. I have always believed in others pushing them to achieve. Meet Lonna White. I learned about her just 5 to 7 years ago. Her mother and I hadn't been in contact since we were 13 years old. We reunited on Facebook a few years back.

MEET LONNA WHITE:

Lonna has aspirations of one day owning three separate businesses. One in drop shipping. Another in travel and a third in real estate. Reconnecting with LaTonya took me back to songs we wrote together as preteens. She remembered the melodies and could recall each line.

Here's a recollection of LaTonya Stewart Boss own words of our childhood memories together:

"Writing these songs were the best childhood memories I can think of with Lonna. I met Lonna at a Pentecostal Church. She was my very first friend I met in El Paso Texas. Lonna was so Cheery and chirper and ALWAYS was adventurous at doing things that involved music.

The first time I sang with Lonna was at a testimonial service. We were 10 years old. We practiced at home and then went in front of the WHOLE church to sing our song. Talk about nervous! Then she talked me into joining the children's choir AND THEN talked to the choir director for ME to LEAD A SONG! We sung a couple of songs in the choir, but I never lead that song because Lonna left that Pentecostal Church and I was too scared to go on.

Leaving that church did not separate us from having a friendship. Both of our parents found another church that they liked and joined. From this church this is where we spent the last 3 years having A LOT of Sunday dinners, every day phone talks, and creating songs at the age of 12.

I moved to Phoenix, AZ when I turned 13. Lonna and I stayed in touch here- and- there the first year but started living the journey God destined in our lives.

Good times those days were. Lonna's childhood friendship meant a lot to me that I named my now 21-year-old daughter after her. The thoughts of our friendship kept me sane during my pregnancy.

Thank you Lonna for allowing God to use you to better his Kingdom with the JOY and LIFE of Music!"

Writing songs with LaTonya hoping one day they would be a hit was the beginning of the unveiling of a theme in my life.

When we finally talked after all the lost years, she still remembered the lyrics, words, and melodies. It brought back so many memories. Children often know what they're passionate about long before adults recognize. Fortunate children are surrounded by adults and support systems who see their voiceprint during their formative years, pull it out, and help develop their gifts.

Honored. Humbled. Moved to tears, but still completely caught off guard by the power of my own voiceprint. I had seen this unveiled in my life before, but never took the time to examine its significance. Defining my own voiceprint seemed impossible at times.

As a child, I questioned, "Where do I fit in?" I knew I was instinctively different, but I didn't know how. I didn't understand why I felt such a burden for others. I didn't understand why I admired and gravitated towards gifts in others but ran from my own. I was innocently fascinated with befriending the shyest person in the room, pulling out a smile and making a friend for life.

Recently, within the last year, I connected with a new friend on Facebook. When I accepted his request, I didn't know where we knew each other from. I only accepted it because we had friends in common. I left Michigan at seven and thought he was a fellow classmate I graduated high school with when we moved back.

A few months back I stopped into our local Walmart for an oil change. It was then I discovered who the man liking and commenting on my posts was. While cashing out, a tall Caucasian man with big brown eyes and the most welcoming smile greeted. He said, "Lonna, it's so good to see you. It's me Chuck. You still look good."

I thought to myself, "Chuck?" Delighted to be speaking in person, we continued. He shared how he often stalked my page and had been wanting to say something. The conversation took a turn. I began to ask him about fellow high school graduates. He appeared clueless. I was dumbfounded. I asked, "Didn't we go to high school together?"

Looking surprised and shocked, he said, "You don't remember me?" I searched aimlessly for an answer hoping a memory came to mind. He said, "Lonna, it's me Chuck from the third grade." I was completely speechless. The third grade?

How could he possibly remember me? He explained why. He revealed he was a socially awkward child, but I was always nice to him. He shared I'd stand up for him and go out of my way to speak. He added, he'd never forget. This was such a lightbulb moment for me because stories like this kept resurfacing in my life again and again.

Friends made jokes and recognized my voiceprint early on. I had no clue.

I struggled in life feeling helpless because I had a huge heart. Everyone knew it. It felt like a cross at times I didn't want to bare. Full of compassion I would cry because of the simplest things. Even when singing in church at times, I 'd start weeping and see someone standing way in the back of the church. I'd make my way over, hugging them and crying with no idea what was wrong. They'd look at me like I was crazy. A week later, someone in their family would die.

I spent days, sometimes weeks at the hospital with families whose loved ones were dying to say a prayer or offer support. I had a history of fighting for the vulnerable, overlooked and underserved. I deeply cared about people and causes most run. It felt like a huge blind spot.

What if I had been able to tap into my voiceprint as a young girl?

What if my perceived weaknesses and shortcomings were seen as strengths?

What if the hidden and unleashed parts of my voiceprint could have helped someone else unleash theirs?

I would have been able to refine and offer my voiceprint in a more profound way to change the world.

As my search to answer these questions continued, I embraced my life in a completely different way. I realized my experiences, challenges and abilities to overcome obstacles could empower, strengthen and unlock others.

I slowly started to own and embrace my voiceprint in a new way. I accepted the parts I had hidden and hated. A pattern and thread of inspiration, hope and compassion emerged.

Many facets of my voiceprint had never been told to a soul.

As a child, I desperately wanted and needed the "voice of affirmation" like so many. I couldn't find it. I looked for it in everything. I searched for it in approval from people. I searched for it in relationships. I searched for it in accomplishments and things.

Born into my family as a middle child, I had been searching for it my entire life. My older sister was accomplished, confident, cool, calm, and collected. She was my childhood hero. I wanted to be just like her. I often compared myself to her and felt second best.

I also longed for the attention everyone gave my younger sister. She could no wrong. She was the cute adorable one and never managed to get in trouble. Everyone's job in the house seemed to be solely to protect her.

My sisters will always have a special place in my heart. Like most, they were there through the hard times. They knew the secrets you couldn't dare utter to a soul. They understood what you couldn't articulate to onlookers and outsiders.

They knew the deep hidden places of my voiceprint.

When I started writing this book, I knew it was a message that needed to get out. I felt stifled and stuck. I wasn't sure I was the one to deliver it or if I even could. I lingered in conflict between the person I portrayed to the world and my true voiceprint.

I hit a point in life where I really began to reflect on where I'd been, where I was, and where I wanted to be. I started to question all the experiences, relationships, and missteps that brought me to my own inner search to find the meaning to life. Had it all been worth it?

As I searched, I realized that like me many have a story or message. The message is so significant it will take more than a podium or speech to deliver. It's a message so big, potent and powerful it must exceed the span of a lifetime. This kind of message needs divine assistance to interrupt time, step in and change the natural occurrence of life to line up to what is, what was, and what's supposed to be.

If you are like me, you probably have found yourself frustrated with life. Do you often analyze the path that brought you to this moment? Are you yearning for more? Do you secretly feel you're living someone else's life and the life you're destined to live is an arm's reach away?

If so, you're probably like I was, in search of the opportunity to release your highest expression and fully unleash your voiceprint.

In my search, I wrestled internally. Parts of my voiceprint had been locked up and tucked away. I wanted to open up and fully share. There were valuable pieces of my existence that made me who I was and couldn't be erased. They were interwoven and an intricate part of who I was.

Was I really ready to let people behind the curtain to deal with the demons of my past? They kept taunting me every day, threatening to keep me tied my past.

I made a profound choice. It's the same choice I challenge you to make today.

I decided to lay aside my fears and inhibitions to boldly declare my voiceprint to the world. Whether in the pages of this book, or painful recollections full of tears in the night, I faced the truth. I had to face the truth of yesterday.

It's the same path that every great leader daring to make a difference in time must take. Will you join me?

If you answered, "yes," I invite you to join me on an introspective voyage. It promises to lead you to higher truths about who you are and what you have to offer the world.

There is a time we all have to face our fears and insecurities. I carried buried insecurities attached to childhood trauma for years. Many didn't truly surface until I reached my lifelong dream of becoming a recording artist followed by my mother's brain aneurysm.

My love for music started as a child. I always loved to sing. I would perform everywhere. My older sister often complained of my incessant need to sing while out shopping with our mother. I somehow believed I'd get discovered like Tina Turner. For some unknown reason, I proudly proclaimed to my family at the age of 5, "When I grow up I'm going to be a star."

No one really believed me. They laughed when I started tap dancing for quarters on the corner of Patwood at the age of 6. I would convince strangers I could tap dance and they'd pay me. I didn't have tap shoes. I didn't have music. In my heart and mind I was singing and tapping because I had a vision. Or did I?

Well, I didn't really have a vision, but I did have a voiceprint.

As I shared earlier, it started to play out at a very young age. My mother would encourage my sisters and I to sing together around the house. I was born into a long line of singers. I became my big sisters mini me. She had an amazing ear for music and the most beautiful voice you'd ever hear. In our family, music ran deep.

My grandfather on my mother's side was a bass singer. He traveled throughout Michigan and Indiana singing in a gospel group called the Union Gospel Mission Quartet which later became the Gospel Tones. My father the late Reverend Eugene E. Hardin was a Baptist preacher who played the piano and could sing too. My aunts, uncles, cousins, and distant relatives could all hold their own. I personally believe I got my love for music, singing and songwriting from my mother, Shirley Jean Clark.

I grew up hearing stories later confirmed by family members about my mother being the original writer behind Motown's "Where did our love go." Family recalls when my mother was in the 8th grade she sent the song in to enter a Motown contest. Motown followed up by sending a contract for permission to record the hit. Being so young, my mother didn't understand contracts and never sent it back. One word was changed. The rest is history.

My mother's love and experience with music started numerous childhood conversations. She repeatedly talked to about:

- Learning the music business
- Copywriting music
- Reviewing contracts, and
- Understanding intellectual property.

When I was old enough to understand about the dangers of running away from home, she later revealed while running away from Michigan to Chicago she wrote, "Runaway Love." She gave the song away to a stranger on a bus and it later became a Temptations hit. It wasn't until years later after her brain aneurysm in 2002 that I actually listened to the words of the song. As a little girl from a small town in Michigan, I totally see how my mother lived the experience.

Born in 1948 in Eau Claire, MI on Frank Farms at a time when many blacks relocated up north to escape the racism of the south, my mother was the oldest daughter of my grandparent's union. My grandma was 14 when she married my granddad. He was 21 and made a living breaking horses and bronc riding.

The story of Margi McKeller and Theotis Clark sudden move from Columbia, Arkansas is tragic. Unlike blacks who left the south looking for a better life, my grandparents fled to save my grandfather's life. A white man made a pass at my grandma. My granddad didn't take it well. Grandpa Clark beat him up and made him pay. In retaliation a bounty was put on his head.

They arrived in the wolverine state with 5 children and nothing else. They started completely over. In the summer when warm, the farm owner allowed them to stay in the hog parlor. In the winter when the pigs needed a place to stay my mom's family stayed in an even tinier house.

Born in 1922 as a Valentine's Day gift to sharecroppers, my grandma, Margie Clark, knew farming well. Census records confirm my great grandparents, George Washington McKeller and Josie Johnson worked on a farm in Columbia trading crops for rent. They could also read and write. At a time when former slaves were forbidden from learning these skills, my great grandparents persevered.

This trait of perseverance followed my grandma to Michigan. My aunts and uncles always reflect on her beautiful, boisterous laugh. She was a strong woman known for fiercely defending her children. She worked tireless to provide what her family needed working up to 3 jobs at a time. She carried the Clark family.

Grandma Clark was also a seamstress. Family members share she could look at a dress, sew it, and duplicate it perfectly without a pattern. I remember being at her house as a little girl fascinated as I watched her crochet. She would try to teach me, but I lacked the patience to learn.

Grandma Clark had three gardens. If you were fortunate enough to be invited in her house, located in the basement were canned fruits, jams, vegetables, and pickled delicacies.

With no formal education, her options for work were few. After raising 10 children, she returned to school to finish her high school diploma once they each graduated.

My own mother continued this trend of perseverance, hard work, caring for her children, and pursuing her education. She didn't have much. What she did always have was a song in her heart and a smile on her face.

A brilliant, beautiful, and virtuous woman, Shirley Jean Clark taught my sisters and I everything we knew about life. She embraced and continued the sharecropping legacy in an entirely new way. She could take almost anything, produce something from it and multiply it's worth.

She was a businesswoman in the early 70s in a male dominated space. At the time, she was raising three young girls as a single mother alone. 20 years her elder, my dad married her at the age of 18. The leading lady to a Pastor, she was married and divorced by age 23. Yet still, she always had a song in her heart and a smile on her face.

My mother was the type of woman who never let you see her sweat. If she was having a bad day, you didn't know. She always had her superwoman cape on when no one was looking and confidently stood up for what she believed.

Shirley Jean Clark was born at a time of civil unrest and protest. She often bragged about participating in the 1963 March on Washington that drew over 250,000 people from across the U.S. She understood what having a voiceprint meant. She knew the cost.

She wore her "crown" and "cape" well. Known as "Lady Gold fingers," everything she touched turned to gold. Growing up, I constantly heard chatter that if my mother and father stayed together they'd be millionaires.

In 1974, I was conceived. At the same time, my parents were getting divorced.

As early as I remember, my mother was heavily involved in the church. She oversaw our church youth department, held teen rallies at LaCrone Park, volunteered for church events and added her voice to every cause she could. I can't remember a time growing up my mom didn't own a business.

I'll never forget at the age of 6, she purchased our first home. When operating expenses became more than she could handle, she shut down her store, "Goldfingers Palace" on Riverview and moved it to our residence at Mt. Olivet.

Today, this may seem pretty normal, but in 1979, my mother took out the garage and put huge glass windows and doors. She turned our home into a legitimate upscale business. My sisters and I learned sales, how to run a cash register, about inventory, and how to count back cash the old-fashioned way.

What gave her the creativity, innovation, resilience, savvy, and ingenuity to do this? Her voiceprint.

My mother had so many admirable qualities. I gravitated to her smile, dream of singing, and songwriting. I wrote my first song at the age of 6. My Aunt still laughs about it to this day. Somehow in 1980, I convinced our Lively Stone church choir director to let me teach it:

Spring is coming, and the Lord is too,

The Lord is coming back for you!

That's it! That's the song in a nutshell. The words rang out and the choir graciously sang the line over and over again. It was a masterpiece!

As we grew older, even though single, my Mom did her best to cultivate our gifts. She encouraged my sisters and I to always be our best. It was an easy thing to do. We looked up to her. She was a Mom to be proud of. Full of drive and ambition, in our household, accomplishment, stick-to-it-ive-ness, and self-sufficiency was the name of the game.

Shirley Jean didn't raise no punks. We grew up with the attitude, "If mommy can do it, so can we!" So, when she announced we were relocating to El Paso, Texas we didn't understand it, but we knew, "Mommy had a plan!" So off we went to our new home. Far away from family. Far away from the norms.

Far away from our family identity or voiceprint!

When we arrived, my mother found a church home to integrate into. Church was a consistent theme in my life. I couldn't get away from it. My father, Reverend Eugene Hardin, was a Baptist preacher christening hundreds of babies. He could deliver a fiery sermon without any notes and helped start 3 churches which still exist over 50 years later. I still get calls from people my father visited in jail, prayed for in the hospital, baptized or mentored in the gospel even after his death on March 11, 2017.

My Grandpa Clark, a known alcoholic and eye wandering philanderer among other things, was also a church deacon and gospel singer. Both were at one time each president of their local NAACP. I always had something to prove and I didn't know why. I didn't need to be better than anyone else, nor did I think I was. I came from a lineage of churchgoers known for affecting change, being a voice, and leaving their mark on the world.

In my early years, I found myself ushering, directing choirs, holding offices, and standing out above my peers. At the age of 10, my mom invested in recording equipment for my sisters and I. Looking back it feels strange. No one knew how to record. My sister 15, and I, age 10 were just excited to have another toy to play with. My mother who believed in our dreams.

We had no clue what we were doing. We enjoyed holding the microphone and singing. At least I did. My sister could sing, play the drums and other instruments too. We formed a group and started traveling to perform.

Music was our escape. Singing was our life. Making melody was our passion.

As a family, my sisters and I also ate, breathed, and slept my mother's business. My mother's drive for business followed her to Texas. She worked full time during the week and ran the store on weekends. Or should I say my sister and I ran it?

We were required to work the store every day after school while my mother worked. At the time, to be honest, I resented it. I didn't know I was learning transferable skills that would last a lifetime.

Throughout my childhood, I continued to carry one simple dream. I wanted to be a star.

I told everyone anywhere I went. I'd sing on street corners performing for change just to get someone else to recognize my gift. In elementary, I rarely paid attention in class. Instead, I'd hummed some song or learn new bars of a ballad. The teacher would be teaching. I'd raise my hand to ask if I could sing in front of the class. After asking enough times most would appease me.

I just knew my love for music and singing would pay off. I would hit the jackpot. Hollywood would somehow find me. This desire only grew. My older sister was really the true singer. I would listen to her and mimic her every move. My family would laugh at me, make fun calling me "tone deaf." I couldn't sing a lick. I didn't care.

I would go in my secret corner and pray. I begged and asked God to please allow me to sing. I remember the day He answered my prayer and it happened. I heard myself sing. I was amazed. This soft, shaking weak voice was now holding notes and hitting octaves I never imagined.

As my confidence grew, my prayers did too. You see I could sing, but I'd freeze up when others were around. My prayers intensified to "Lord, let me sing in front others. Let them listen to me."

This was how I spent most of my childhood and adolescence. Hoping, singing, believing, praying, and seeing myself as a star.

I'd seen faith work so many times. I decided to give my life to Christ at any early age. My life didn't suddenly change. I didn't stop doing every crazy thing. It was a decision I made every day over and over again. There were times I didn't feel like a Christian, look like it or make choices that aligned with my faith. It was a part of my journey. and later, I'd discover, a part of my voiceprint.

When I found myself in trouble or at a crossroads in life, God was there. I finally decided if I'd fall, I'd fall forward. After falling on my face again and again, I decided to recommit in a new way at the age of 21. I wish I could say that was the day my life became perfect. I wish I could tell you I never made poor choices or wrong decisions again, but it would be a lie.

At the age of 19, I attempted to commit suicide. Living on college campus, I'd given in to some temptations I was too embarrassed to tell a soul. One night, alone and depressed, I decided to try to take my own life. Thank God, He had other plans. After having my stomach pumped at a local hospital, my mother asked why. My response, "I wanted to be saved."

After that night, I promised God no matter how hard things became, I'd never do that again. I wouldn't be tricked into discounting my own worth and existence. Over the next few years, I inched my way closer and closer to God. I left old friendships and mindsets behind. I immersed myself in activities to help find a clearer path. I found a church family, joined and spent the early part of my adulthood on fire. I volunteered my time, started directing the youth choir, sang on the praise team, and later became a full-time employee.

My dreams of being a star faded in my new-found way of life. At that point, I didn't want anything to come between my relationship with God. I silenced the voices of my past and started embracing who I was. I studied scripture in a new profound way. My prayer life went to an entirely new place.

This was the time of my life. I truly had a "new song" and a "new sound."

Then, it happened. My Pastor challenged me and said, "I know you love to sing" but you have to at least go back to school and get your associate degree." Huh? What? I was puzzled.

Didn't he know I hated school? It was boring. I found my passion in other places. Since I respected his opinion and voice-print, I took his advice. I returned to school, only to hear my dreams knocking again. I started taking music classes and singing even more.

I performed the Star-Spangled Banner at Kellogg Auditorium opening for General Colin Powell. This was a major turning point for me. All of a sudden, the stakes were higher, and my confidence became weaker.

In 1999, I recorded my first solo project, "Praise Him." This is where the spotlight turned on and I was rudely awakened. Singing and passion have to be more than a hobby. Up until that time, I had sung for "fun," as a means of "healing" or "personal release."

Most didn't know this was all I wanted in life. Fear arose. "What if I didn't have what it took?" When I performed, my voice would tighten. I struggled through each song. Anyone who has performed in church knows it's the toughest crowd. I doubted my own gift, purpose, and wondered if singing was even God's will.

I began to doubt and question my voiceprint.

All my shortcomings, self-doubt, and fears showed up. If I wanted a career of longevity it would take more. Performing in front of audiences required another level of discipline. I couldn't just be pretty and look the part. I had to do more than play the part. I actually had to be and sound the part. I had to "live the part."

Standing before crowds suddenly became nerve wrecking.

Would the audience know I didn't know how to hold the mic right? I never had voice lessons. I didn't have a stylist or makeup artist. No manager. No vocal coach.

Every insecurity I ever had suddenly magnified. I would get up on stage and freeze. I couldn't feel the song. I was so fear stricken. I felt so paralyzed by my own inabilities. I'd tightly close my eyes scared to open them. If I did I 'd see every movement, expression and face in the audience. In return, surely, they could also see me.

Each time I got up to sing in front of a crowd, it required me to open my heart.

Over time I realized this was a painful, excruciating process. There were areas of my heart I didn't want to open. There were painful memories and secrets I wanted no one to see. There were parts of my life, character and weaknesses that held me hostage. I couldn't explain them to soul. They had snatched my voice and hit the mute button.

I couldn't spiritualize it (although I tried). All I could do was hide, run away in shame and hope no one could see, feel or hear the pain I was masking behind my voice and song. This eventually worked. The more I hid and closed my heart, the more the crowd stopped listening, cheering and applauding.

Mainly, because I stopped showing up and taking the stage. I quit allowing myself to appear. Rather than show my weakness, vulnerability and imperfection, I made a choice to walk away from what I loved most. I gave up hope. I gave up singing. I gave up my song.

I started to resent and withdraw from my voiceprint.

Everyone knew the strong parts of Lonna. The encourager. The friend. The loving Lonna. The happy go lucky Lonna. The sing down the halls Lonna. The act like she has it all together Lonna, but no one knew my pain.

They didn't know the Lonna who was molested twice between the ages of 6 and 10. They didn't know the Lonna who came from a family line of secrets, incest, alcoholism and molestation. A family where when you went to family gatherings you knew something was off but couldn't quite put your finger on exactly what it was.

No one knew the Lonna who used to be awakened at night with a tap on the door by our mother instructing us to sneak out the window to meet her at the corner store. My alcoholic stepfather was having another episode.

Did anyone know the real Lonna? Yes, me.

I was the same child who at the age of 6 ended up in a vehicle where my Mom drove us downtown. She told us to wait in the car while she made a run. Minutes later my sisters and I were startled. My mother ran out of a downtown bar, hurried into the car and began to drive away.

Suddenly we noticed another car driving into us. It was my drunk stepfather determined to take us down. He crashed directly into us. A tiny piece of glass stuck in my forehead for days. I still have the mark. If you look close enough you can see it. It didn't bleed. The glass never pierced my skin.

This incident is where I picked up my first nickname, "The miracle child."

Did the onlookers in the audience see the Lonna kidnapped along with her sister at the age of 7? It was my birthday. I'll never forget my Stepfather took my sister and I to Denny's and drove us around Michigan. After driving for hours, we started to wonder if we'd ever see our mother again. To get back home, I lied. I said there was a chicken bone stuck in my throat. My inebriated stepfather took us to the hospital. I informed the police. My mother was called.

No. No one knew that Lonna. It was the Lonna I was afraid to introduce to anyone and wanted no one to see. You see my life has never been ordinary or conventional. Therapists and psychologists would call it dysfunctional. Not just any dysfunctional but "highly" dysfunctional. Somehow my sisters and I always managed to function.

Like my mother, we smiled through the pain and always had a song in our heart. Few knew what we lived through. We hid it with our song. It stayed hidden for most of my life. I blocked it. It didn't seem like a huge problem until I became older and started dating. I desperately desired a knight and shining armor to rescue me. I desired someone to take all the painful memories away.

Most men complained about my guardedness. They didn't understand why it was so hard for me to trust. They were confused at why I ran from intimacy, lacked balance in relationships, and often played hard to get. I had a huge, passionate, romantic heart, but very few got close enough to see.

I can attribute this to growing up without a father. The late Reverend Eugene Hardin was brilliant and charming. He served in the Air Force and Navy at a time when black men were given the rank of 2nd class. Many lied about their age and hid their true identities to get into the military.

My father was admired and loved. Favor followed him. I remember his ability to swoon women. They were ensnared. When we visited his churches, they catered to us. We were Reverend Hardin's children. Most wanted to be the next First Lady.

Seeing the power my father had to get what he wanted when he wanted, mixed with the trauma of an alcoholic stepfather and dark family secrets, colored my perspectives. Sadly, no one could walk my journey or understand to help me unblur the lines.

Yes, this Lonna I longed to let out to let put. I wanted badly to stand on the highest pinnacle of a mountain, open my mouth to sing and let the world hear my REAL voiceprint, but pride and religion got in the way.

Always optimistic. Always compassionate and helping others while smiling through pain. But then the question arose. Can they even handle the truth? Could I handle the truth?

I mean the hatred, backbiting and gossiping I dealt with in the church was no better. I can honestly tell you there were seasons, sometimes years I went and hid. I couldn't bring myself to step into a church. Too many painful memories. I needed nothing else to add to my trauma and pain.

Just when you think you're healing and strong, here comes someone else with an opinion or lie putting their mouth on situations where they don't belong. I like to call them Sister and Brother "No clue." No clue what you've been through. No clue how to help. No clue who you really are. No clue how to really add value to your life. Always an opinion but never a clue.

So, after serving relentlessly in ministry to hide my shame and mask the pain, I ran again.

During this time, I questioned who I was. I questioned the motivation behind my desire to sing. I ignored the voiceprint of my parents and lessons of the past. I forgot the many times God used singing and music in my life to bring me through really hard times. I blocked out so painful childhood memories completely tuning them out. I erased each with melodies from a song.

My first recording never went anywhere. That said, I learned a lot in the process. We met with Nashville distribution companies, radio stations, and industry experts who shared advice on what was needed to take the project to the next level.

I did get eventually complete my associate degree. Once I realized I didn't have to be intimidated by going back to school, I pushed ahead to do even more. I enrolled in the Bachelor of Arts program majoring in Theatre with a minor in Musical Theatre. I auditioned and was accepted.

So excited and happy, I was on my way to "Living My Song." I was on my way to realizing my dream. Unexpectedly during this season of my life, something crazy happened. My world was rocked. My voice slowly felt like it had been stolen and snatched. My confidence was shaken again!

October 2002, my mother had a brain aneurysm. It ruptured. She also suffered a stroke on each side of her brain. When I received the call, I was devastated. A 52- year old strong, beautiful, enterprising businesswoman and family matriarch, she now fought for her life in intensive care.

At the time, we didn't know what this would mean for our family's future. She was my closest friend. Even worse, two days before, a family argument had taken place. Something so trivial caused my mother to ignore phone calls for days. The woman we depended on all our lives shut down. This was absolutely unheard of. She was the most loving, forgiving, caring soul you would ever meet. She normally didn't let anything bother her. I left message after message.

Now this was happening. What if I never heard my mother's

voice again? What if she died before I made it into town? What if the woman who always pulled me through didn't make it?

I was at a loss for words. The very wind was knocked out of me. There was no time for an action plan. I spent days, weeks and months driving back and forth on the highway to see her. I spent months in prayer interceding for my mother and family.

It was a very tumultuous time. I lost friends. I lost interest in things that used to bring me joy. I didn't care about anything or anyone. I didn't even care about my own needs. All I cared about was my mother getting better.

In 2003, five months after her brain aneurysm, my mother was released. Our family thought we would finally be able to rest but our caregiving journey just began. Five months and six years later after navigating new waters and slowly making it through one of our family's first major storms, we learned the news. My mother was exhibiting strange behaviors. My sisters and I didn't know whether to step in and do something or let her continue to enjoy independence. Deep down within we all knew something was terribly wrong.

My mother lost her ability to walk. We tried rehab and outpatient therapy with little success. Then, after reaching the point of no return, we found her diagnosis. The doctor said had Vascular dementia. "Vascular dementia?"

At 28, no one handed over a manual to explain what this meant for my mother and family. No one told us we would have to cope with a brand-new reality alone. Hurt, loss, depression, and fear all came at once. We carried the weight of guilt, responsibility and the need to do what we needed for my Mother's sake.

I lost my desire to sing. I lost a lot during that time. Then, it happened. I was attending a youth conference given by a local church. I attended to help out a single mother who had to work. I developed a great relationship with her kids and decided to take them. I went, attended and ended up meeting what I needed most, a good friend.

During the Friday night meeting I met a handsome musician. He played behind me while I sang. We laughed, joked and exchanged numbers. We talked on the phone, talking about God and sharing our love of music. This was a pleasant distraction. Something to take my mind off all I felt I lost, the pain, the fear of the unknown and the future.

During this time, I started and continued a new relationship. Happy to have an opportunity to not have to always "be strong" and to be able to "let down my hair," I started withdrawing from my church family unintentionally and blaming the world. It was a hard time. I pushed through it all. I managed my own personal crisis, a long-distance relationship, and the changing dynamics of our family.

In 2005, just months short of graduating with my degree, I found myself pregnant. After moving to Indiana to be closer to the love of my life, I relocated home to start life over as a single mother. Did I mention I was 5 months pregnant when I returned and had just released my first internationally released recording project?

I had 4 songs being played in France and around the world. Named #17 on the International Top 30 along with Jay Z,

John Legend, and Janet Jackson, I was featured on the top 150 gospel radio stations throughout the US. The record company sent me back to Michigan to have the baby with family and friends. I was supposed to return to the road once the baby was born to continue to promote the cd.

Originally, I signed a deal that promised to start recording my full album in April of 2006, but the label threatened to not record it unless I promoted the compilation first without promise of compensation.

I felt like a complete failure. I prayed for this all my life.

I didn't want to grow up telling my daughter stories of what could have been. I heard stories like this from my mother all my life. I wanted to have something of credible substance to leave. I wanted to give her a legacy she could be proud of. I'd blown it.

I moved back to Michigan humiliated, devastated, embarrassed and a hundred pounds larger than when I left. No one expected me to get pregnant, not even me. The biggest advocate for abstinence, I was someone youth admired. I failed my parents. I failed myself. I failed my daughter. I failed my dreams.

The record company still wanted me to hit the road. I felt I needed to make a decision. Would I own up to my mistakes? Would I take care of my daughter to do all I could to make sure she had a better life? Or would I selfishly act like it was all about me and my dreams?

I made a decision to step away, go back to work and raise my child. When I returned, I hid from it all. I withdrew into a dark depression and gained a tremendous amount of weight. I stopped caring. Why should I?

I became:

- A work at home mom for 12 years
- I stopped singing
- I made excuses for why I hadn't accomplished my dreams
- I kept telling myself the life I longed for would never happen
- I beat myself up again and again
- I stopped hoping
- I stopped believing
- I gave up on me

In 2008, I attempted to take care of my mother. It was something I couldn't do alone. As a single mom, I thought about how many other women like me gave up on themselves and their dreams. I started to see things in a bigger light. Most single mothers couldn't even think about leaving a legacy for their children. Many were stuck in survival mode making it happen day to day just to do what they needed to take care of their kids.

I stopped thinking like a victim and started strategizing on what I could do to help.

How could I change the trajectory for my child and others?

How could I use all I had been through to give back and honor my parents legacy?

Ultimately through introspection and reflection, I made a choice to do something with my song while I had time. I found the beauty and rhythm I lost to dance again. I stopped searching outside myself for answers and relied on the strength within. I started to discover the themes shared by both my parents and threaded in my voiceprint that held me together through some of my lowest times.

They are:

- **FAITH** - Faith can move mountains. With faith, you can overcome anything. Nothing is impossible.
- **LOVE** - Love can and will conquer all. Love others as you want to be loved.
- **HOPE** - As long as there is hope there is the chance for a better or different outcome. Never give up. Keep believing.
- **COMPASSION** - Humanity connects us all. Compassion can heal.
- **PRAYER** - Ask. Believe. Receive.
- **HEALING** - Nothing is beyond love's repair.
- **SUFFERING** - Suffering opens our heart to the pains of others. It humbles us and makes us strong.
- **SONSHIP** - We are created in the image of a loving father who never wants to see us fail and is there to pick us back up when we do. He desires for us to reflect Him in all we do.

- **SONG** - Music and song is a tool to release our voiceprint in the earth. Once sung, it's never taken away. It must be set free and allowed to roam the universe to touch whatever it pleases.

The path of forgiveness started. I woke up to new realities, new stories, and new voices inspiring me to encourage me to press on to discover hidden gems waiting in my voiceprint ready to be unmuted and unlocked.

Think about the voices keeping you bound to what could have been instead of what can be. Time to move forward and unlock your voiceprint!

Identify two painful memories you have been unable to release or share? Why? Do you believe this stops you from fully unleashing your voiceprint? If so, how?

1) ____

2) ____

CHAPTER 4

Unmute Me

Ever been on a conference call? You're totally into the conversation. You finish saying something really good and are pat yourself on the back. You notice no one on the other end responds.

Maybe you finished a long webinar anxiously wait to ask the very question you attended for. Suddenly, Q&A is over. You heard the moderator call your name. You began asking your question. Now, it seems you've been ignored? You frantically start checking your headset and computer. You surprisingly look down and realize you've been muted the entire time. No one has heard a word you said.

For many of us, this is how life has been. We're carrying a message but have been unable to deliver it. The mute button somehow got pushed on our device. Even worse, it was pushed at the very time we were adamantly passionate about what it was we wanted the world to hear us say. We knew what we were about.

When I first wrote, "Melody's Song and the City of the Voice Snatchers" it was a story written to help single parents and children who lacked strong support systems. However, even greater, it was the story of my own life.

In the story, a little girl named Melody lives in a city powered by music. Every 30 days someone writes the town song to power the city for 30 days. Melody knows one day her song will be chosen. Every time she goes to sing, something crazy happens. She opens her mouth to sing and frogs come out. Another time, she opens her mouth to sing and her feet run backwards the other direction.

The kids are always making fun of her, but her mom keeps telling her she's a special little girl. One day at school, a talent show is announced, whoever wins gets to power the city for 30 days. Melody knows this is her chance. She excitedly tells her mother who begs her not to do it. What do you think Melody does?

She auditions, but when she opens her mouth to sing, nothing comes out. Instead, she opens her mouth to sing and several butterflies come out with a huge hand that scratches the chalkboard from top to bottom. The kids laugh and make fun of her. Melody is devastated. She says she'll never sing again.

That's when her mother tells her the secret. When she was born it was foretold she'd be the girl with the golden voice. That's when the voice snatchers started attacking the city kidnapping the singers to power their own dark city. To protect her, her mother took her voice and had it sealed away. I won't tell you the ending, but it's a powerful story about self-love, self-awareness, self-confidence and self-identity. The story resonates with audiences around the world.

I wish I could tell you the idea just came to me one day. The truth is, I was that little girl desperately wanting to sing. I felt I had a song that could change the world, but someone walked by and pressed mute. Voice snatchers stripped my voice at critical times in my life. It was like the recurring dream I had as a little girl kept repeating itself. It haunted me for years. I still remember it like it was yesterday. I had it so many times and couldn't get the images or feelings out of my mind.

When we were little, my sister and I watched the original Incredible Hulk tv series. It was just another show or, so I thought. It wasn't until I dreamed my first nightmare that the show caused crippling fear to strike my heart.

It happened the same each time. Incredible Hulk would break down our front door. We would take off running in every direction. I always found myself in a closet or under the bed feeling safe.

As I sat there quietly breathing while also holding my breath hoping not to be discovered, in walked the ugly green Monster. He would *always* find me. When he would, I'd open my mouth to scream. Each and every time, nothing came out! It's like my voice was silenced. Someone hit the mute button when I needed my voice most.

I'd wake up panic stricken to discover it was just a dream. It never made the feeling of being fear stricken, unable to move and unable to speak go away. Many have this feeling every day, *only it is not a dream*. Something traumatic or unexpected in life happened and hit mute.

The Merriam-Webster Dictionary offers the following definitions for the word mute:

1. Unable to speak; lacking the power of speech.
2. Characterized by absence of speech; such as
3. Remaining silent, undiscovered, or unrecognized
4. A device attached to or inserted into a musical instrument to soften or altar it's tone.

Our voiceprint was meant to distinguish us and set us apart of from others. For the purpose of this chapter, we'll go with the third definition:

Remaining silent, undiscovered, or unrecognized.

Many live life below the radar, undetected and not truly walking in purpose. Some because of age and gender. Some because of poor choices and environment.

Most because they have failed to recognize their voiceprint.

Others have been waiting for someone to believe in them to support their dreams. Some simply second guess whether they have what it takes to really make it. Excuses, circumstances, inaction, lack of education or opportunities leave them muted, unable to speak and move forward.

Is that you? Do you silently feel you're living someone else's life not fully experiencing the life you were destined to live? Can you think of a time you really felt you were the best person for the job or had the answer everyone needed but didn't speak up because of fear?

What has your life muzzled? What do you secretly want to do or say but haven't mastered the courage to try?

Your voiceprint is a compass. If used it can guide your life to the path of power, freedom, creativity, and purpose. When unleashed, it carries everything you need within.

Maybe you feel because of race, class, or status you're not destined to release your voiceprint. I know this feeling well. It's an easy trap to fall into. Thinking back to my days as a little girl in El Paso, Texas I'm reminded how easy it is to remain *"undiscovered or unrecognized"* to those around you. Maybe they can't see or interpret the value of your voiceprint.

I remember my days being educated in a traditional public-school setting. I felt the trauma of being overlooked, discounted, and told how to feel and think. I lived this reality every day.

It was February 1984 and our second year living in El Paso, TX. We were celebrating Black History Month. The only black child in the class, my teacher, Mrs. Butler, asked me to read. My voice started to quiver and shake. The class stared silently. My nervous voice felt unempowered and afraid.

I began to read about slavery and the torment black slaves endured. Tears filled my eyes. They began dripping quickly from my face. I tried to wipe them and keep going. They wouldn't stop. Finally, I got up and ran out of the class.

Mrs. Butler obviously shaken by my outburst, ran out behind me. She compassionately gazed in my eyes and asked, "Lonna, what's wrong?" I innocently replied, "Why is the only thing you read about black people is that they were slaves?"

She didn't have an answer. You see even at age 10, I knew that was not my voiceprint. It didn't characterize the goodness, humanity, tenacity, hope and resilience I'd seen in myself or my own family and friends.

I couldn't connect to that voiceprint. I didn't identify with it.

Sometimes situations, circumstances, people or things work to define who you are and place limitations on what you have to offer the world. In these cases, it's easy to allow something outside ourselves to "mute" or muzzle what we truly stand for or believe. It's in these times we must make a conscious decision to exclaim our voiceprint and loudly proclaim, "Unmute me."

No one can declare this for us. It's something we have to boldly decide to do regardless of ridicule, tension, or retaliation we face.

Recently I had a conversation with friends. We had a discussion about history makers who contributed to the underground railroad or made a huge impact on our world. One friend said she was tired of focusing on those who impacted the past, but not on those making an impact today.

The conversation was quite enlightening and inspiring. That said, I pointed out, one notable difference. Many like Sojourner Truth, Harriet Tubman, Frederick Douglass, or Reverend Martin Luther King, Jr. died for what they believed.

Who's willing to die selling out to the sound of their voiceprint? Is that you?

It's easy to live life status quo and remain muted when no one knows about the perspectives, passions, and positions we carry inside. Living life on mute allows us to remain unnoticed and go undetected playing it safe, waiting for the next history maker to be born.

Why not you? Why not now? Will you stand up to be a history maker, world shaker, or game changer?

If you're like most adults, you start off believing in the power of your own voiceprint. Think back to when you were young. You believed anything was possible. Remember how you felt? Do you remember everything you dreamed? What happened between now and then to change your focus, passion, and mind?

Many experienced a setback or unexpected trauma in life that muzzled their potential. No one told them they possess the power within to change the direction of their lives. Instead they're waiting for someone to take the muzzle off to release them into purpose. These individuals spend days and nights with regrets resenting what could have been instead of dreaming about the power in their hands.

You can't afford to wait for anyone. The person or thing you're waiting for, may be the very person or thing that understands the threat you pose once your voiceprint is unleashed.

A voiceprint can alter time.
A voiceprint can change the course of a nation.
A voiceprint can influence people.

A voiceprint can destabilize the norms.

A voiceprint even when whispered can be felt across the world. Ask the wind. It can't speak with words, but still carries a sound that can shift atmospheres, change direction, and carry elements from one place to the next. The wind is powerful enough to destroy homes if mixed with rain. It can uproot trees, make waves, and impact resources.

What can a person do who recognizes the power of their voiceprint?

Which muzzle has you stifled, stuck, and unable to pursue all in your heart. What makes you feel powerless and muted? What would your life look if you fully expressed your voiceprint? Who would be positioned around you cheering you on?

We all go through seasons of feeling like we're muted, unable to speak, misunderstood and unable to move. It's in these times our other senses are tested and tried. They become much keener and more acute.

Seasons of being mute can work for us or against us. It's all in perspective.

When you find yourself in these seasons it's important to tap into what's working. Becoming self-aware, locating yourself and identifying where you are can be critical to the next stop on your journey.

This season is where you stop looking outside for validation. Stop venting to others to give you sight and clarity. Tune out the noise of your surroundings. Tap into your own inner strength and voiceprint. Although uncomfortable, being in a season on mute brings greater satisfaction when you truly unleash your voiceprint. You gain the confidence to believe in you when no one else will.

This season will also bring a great deal of persecution. You will want to defend yourself. Be careful not to go into self-preservation mode. It's easy to do. *Accept what comes and stay focused!*

Don't spend time explaining your journey. Embrace the chatter. Embrace the vulnerability of exposing your true voiceprint. Find other ways to communicate your creativity, vision, future, and dreams. Outlive and outgrow the persecution. Remember what living life on mute felt like. Keep showing up to articulate your highest goals and dreams.

This is usually the stage just before you fully cross over into new reality of living life in your 6th sense to transcend opinions, circumstances, limiting beliefs, and expectations.

It's time to take serious inventory. Have a conversation within. What brought you to this place? What is holding you back. It's your time. Declare to the universe and world, "Unmute me."

ACTION STEPS

Make a list of the people, self-limiting beliefs, patterns and things in your life that make you feel like your life has been muted. Why?

1) ______________________________

2) ______________________________

3) ______________________________

4) ______________________________

5) ______________________________

CHAPTER 5

Finding Your Unique voiceprint

Your voiceprint can unlock time, opportunities, potential and people. It has the power to change the entire direction of the human race with just one command. Sadly, many are living without understanding its power and how it can transform their own lives and others.

When you find your voiceprint, your life will operate like an Amazon Echo. It will take you to the exact destination you command it to go. You won't need to use Google Maps or MapQuest to get there taking twists and turns.

Your voiceprint will attract the right people, places, spouses, businesses, and opportunities to you. You will walk in dimensions in time specifically designed for you and aligned with who you are. You'll walk in the circles you were destined to without feeling less than, inferior, or you don't belong.

The beginning of any journey starts with locating yourself in proximity to where you want to go. Only then can you determine what's needed and missing to get you to your final destination. In the journey of finding, embracing and using your voiceprint, I've found people start the journey in one of four "places":

- ***Voice Search***: you know you have a voice but have not identified it and are you are looking OUTSIDE yourself to others to define it.
- ***Voice Recognition:*** you recognize your voice, but you haven't quite started listening to it yet.
- ***Voice Identification*** - You have identified your voice, but are stuck and have not defined your song
- ***Voice Activation:*** you know your voice, you know your song, you are ready to step out and use it. You need a coach to support you on your journey to help you amplify it.

When I speak to audiences around the world about the power of using their voice and finding their "voiceprint," it astonishes me that many adults don't understand the concept. Few have been taught how to tap into their inner strengths and unique attributes to live their best life and "Live their song." Many can relate when hearing gurus or marketers tell them they need to tell their story or define their brand, but a voiceprint is much bigger than that.

Discovering your voiceprint requires looking at your life in its totality and recognizing the themes, people, experiences, and "aha moments" that have shaped who you are. It embodies your essence and core values.

It's not just the part of you that you allow others to see. It's who you are even when no one's looking. It's the deep impression you "want" to leave in people's soul or mind. It's the trail of success and failures you have lived through. It's the powerful legacy you will leave for years to come. It's the song that emanates from your life with all its ups and downs, twists and turns.

When the stage lights are off and crowds are gone, what masks do you take off? What problems in the world or worries about the future bring you tears and make you weep? What are the lessons you've learned in life that are hard for others to face but need to be heard?

So many passively decide to "fake it until they make it." Some only put their best foot forward so others can perceive them in a better light. In a social media and success driven age, there is definitely value in projecting and portraying your best. On the other hand, what many often miss is the opportunity to not just talk about the success, but to also share the authentic story of their suffering.

Many don't equate suffering to success, but the truth is they go hand in hand.

In our growth, we must decide to not just focus outwardly to look the part, but also do the internal work that allows us to maintain success overtime. This helps us to integrate discipline, integrity, authenticity, perseverance and other qualities into our character. Once interwoven into our character this becomes a part of our voiceprint.

Technology companies are catching on to the power of an authentic voiceprint. They've tapped into the secret that is now making them billions of dollars in sales. It's time we catch on too.

In my consulting work with Silicon Valley startups I see the value of sweat equity through the eyes of venture capitalists. These principles once discovered turn into strong intellectual property, patents, and billion-dollar deals.

See your unique experiences, triumphs, and valuable lessons learned as sweat equity others to share with the world. What problems in the world could be solved because of you. Your voiceprint carries the answer to some of the world's toughest problems.

The "sweat equity" we put in on our journey to finding and unleashing our voiceprint is invaluable. It pays residuals and dividends. It makes our voiceprint much more effective, lasting, and profound. Others gain a deeper respect and reverence for our unique voiceprint that allowed us to overcome obstacles, defy odds, and persevere in the face of great challenges.

As we swiftly move into the digital age, technology is taking over. Coding, robotics, augmented reality, machine automation, and virtual reality will be the trends of the future. These technologies are quickly replacing real everyday human interactions. Practices like neuro-linguistic programming are becoming widely accepted and adopted. Even marketers are finding ways to replace real live human emotion with bots, emoticons and hashtags.

Siri, Alexa and Google Home have already caught on to the principles I am sharing in this book. What is it that Apple, Google, and Amazon understand that 99% of the world does not?? What keeps products like Amazon Echo and the Apple

Siri capabilities so high in demand? These companies and technologies capture and realize the power of a voiceprint!

They've figured out how to capture the voice, tap into the brilliance of voice command, and use a person's voice to transcribe spoken words to paper and perform voice search. Although these amazing devices can capture the voice, use voice command and duplicate the voice, they can never create it.

God in His infinite wisdom predestined who you are and who you would be. He assigned each individual their own unique voiceprint. He placed it within you and gave you the power to speak, create, and live from it.

The key is you who must claim it, possess it, own it and use it!

Name three experiences in life you have that can be used as "sweat equity" to help someone else that you have persevered through.

1) ____

2) ____

3) ____

CHAPTER 6

Lost your voice? Still Searching?

Have you come to a place in life where you feel like you've lost your voice? Or do you often feel as if you don't fit or belong? You keep searching for answers outside yourself but haven't found the answer you need.

Do you sometimes find yourself in environments that do not reflect your future goals or where you want to be? Or do you find yourself surrounded by people, circumstances or things that don't represent you at your best?

Are you in a dead-end job that doesn't align with your personal values or who you really are? Stuck in a city you don't want to be in but aren't sure of your next move?

If you answered yes, to any of these questions it sounds like you are in the **Voice Search** stage. You know you have a voiceprint but haven't identified it. In voice search, you feel and know there's a void. All the things you worked so hard for seem insignificant because something's missing.

You say things like:

- What's my purpose?

- There's more to life than this!
- Why do I feel like I'm missing out on life?

If you are at this stage, you look OUTSIDE to others and material things to define you:

- Your career
- Your salary
- Your relationship
- Your children
- Your family
- Your friends

Your voice lies *WITHIN* and until you tap into who you are at the core – you will forever be in search mode.

In the Voice Search phase, you're still searching for the message that resonates. You may be looking for it in money, success, friends, clothes, makeup, jewelry, alcohol, partying, sex and drugs.

Voice searchers are going from conference to conference, reading blog to blog looking for answers. You haven't found your own path or realized your true worth. You haven't fully discovered your voice. You're searching without direction or focus.

Voice searchers know they are at this stage because they feel stuck in the same pattern doing the same thing over and over. You may feel stagnant and lack movement in life. You accept status quo living beneath your potential believing one day you'll magically reach your destination. You don't know where to begin.

As a little girl growing up in a single parent home, I often longed for the "voice of affirmation" from my father. I loved my mother deeply. She was a God fearing, strong, resilient, loving, nurturing, and beautiful woman. I looked up to her. Even with all those qualities, I still needed to hear my father's voice.

I was searching for the voice I knew I needed to show me more of who I was. I needed to hear a voice that reminded me where I came from and where I was going. Fathers carry identity. They have the ability to see something in a child and bring it out of them. They are protectors, providers, and have the ability to name a thing.

According to some cultures and customs, the father has the first right to name their firstborn child. For those that are bible scholars, when you look at the story of creation on the 6th day was when God created animals. It was Adam who named them. God put an innate quality in man to be able to look at something, identify it and name it.

Within my own circle and among my male friends, I am often even amazed at how many can think 10 to 20 years ahead when planning for their careers, families, children and future.

One of my clients is a music licensing client who has been in the industry for over 20 years. They have licensed music to networks like NBC, CBS, and CNN. They have also done music for Kraft Group of the New England Patriots and some of their music has even been featured previously on the Oprah Show.

My client consists of a two-man team that owns about 7 patents and counting. One day I was running an idea by them I had for a new music app. They are both quite gracious and quietly chuckled to themselves. What they shared in the next 30 minutes was absolutely mind-blowing. They shared how they had been able to create new technology, software, and foster new ideas. It was their ability to think years in advance, identify the invention and name it before anyone else.

The team spoke about their journey of success. Every patent, every invention, and every discovery are directly tied to their ability to hear and follow their own voice and gut instinct.

They weren't looking to some other entity to affirm their ideas or path. As a matter of fact, when I was researching whether or not to take on the client, I checked out their online social profiles. There was very little information given. One of the pair only had one word to describe them and it was "autodidactic." Embarrassingly, at the time I didn't even know what it meant. I had to look it up. It means "self-taught."

I also have had the opportunity to see several success stories unfold in the lives of former classmates and friends. One, former classmate, Derek Jeter, recently retired from the New York Yankees. He made his mark on history and will go as one of the greatest baseball players of our time.

In high school, Derek was always very focused. He was awesome, down to earth, and very laid back. What I remember most was his ability to stay humble but still follow his own path. Many chimed in on his future and what he should do, but what I saw was a trend of knowing his own destiny and own voiceprint. He wasn't searching outside himself or swayed by the influence of peers and those around him.

One other amazing success story, is the climb of a dear friend's son, John Legend. He will leave a legacy of being one of the most brilliant businessmen, prolific songwriters, social justice advocate, entertainer and voiceprints of our times. I had the opportunity to meet him at the age of 27. I had been friends with his father for quite some time.

When I first began pursuing a music career, his father supported and purchased several CDs. As our friendship evolved, he told me about his son, who at the time was known as "John Stephens." He shared his son lived on the east coast and also was pursuing a music career. He then gave me a copy of John's first independently recorded project.

I played that cd again and again. I let youth I mentored hear it and everyone had an opinion. Between 2000 and 2001, John's father introduced us via email. One thing I remember, is how straight and to the point he was. He was focused. He was tuned in to the sound of his own voiceprint. Years later, his focus, discipline, and vision paid off. He knew who he was. He wasn't searching.

Knowing both backstories is even more impressive than what they've. Each had fathers who recognized their giftings or voiceprint at young ages and helped them to believe in themselves, take their dreams seriously, refine their craft and reach their destination.

Growing up without a father in the home, or that voice of affirmation I spoke of earlier, always left me searching. I searched for attention. I searched for acceptance. I searched for approval. I searched for someone to identify with my voiceprint. What I often found was frustration, rejection, ridicule, persecution, and sometimes shame.

This led me on a downward spiral of creating a pattern of needing to look for something I felt I didn't have. I would see celebrities, mentors, and peers I looked up to doing amazing things, and it would give me just a glimpse what life could look like if I found my own voice.

Others believed in me, but I couldn't quite find the confidence I needed to believe in myself. I kept searching until finally I looked behind and found a trail of perceived failures, disappointments, regrets, and memories of should have, could have, would have. It wasn't until I decided to stop waiting on others for approval and support. It was then I began to produce and create out of my voiceprint.

Can you relate? Have you wanted to do something impactful in life, but don't know what or how? You've been told you were great at this or can see yourself doing something amazing but can't quite figure out how to get there or connect the dots. It's time to stop searching for answers outside and find your voiceprint.

CHAPTER 7

Listen to The Sound of Your Own Voice. Recognize Your Worth.

In **voice recognition**, you have made it beyond the search stage and you now know your own voice. When you hear it, you know it belongs to you. You see someone speaking or doing something and it resonates with who you are. You exclaim, "*That's what I've always wanted to do!*"

Or you meet an author at an event and go home and start to dream of writing your own book. You recognize your voice, but haven't developed the habit of listening to it and tuning in.

At this stage you say things like:

- I'm too old to live out my childhood dreams.
- My children and family come first.
- No one wants to hear my story.
- Who cares about my voice.

At this stage, we make excuses and develop reasons not to pursue our own voiceprint.

What excuses are you telling yourself? The quicker you let them go, the faster you create the life you've always dreamed of. This requires taking time to listen to your inner voice, the lessons your life has been attempting to teach you and going through the process of deep introspection.

Listening to the sound of your own inner voice is a skill.

So many times, we take in the sounds of others voices in our lives. We may be still repeating a lie we heard years ago that we will never amount to anything or will always live below the poverty line. We may believe that lie that we have to be married to accomplish our dreams or make more money.

What sounds have you allowed yourself to take in or voices from the past have you chosen to listen to?

As a vocalist, I've always been intrigued with sound. Sound is about absorption. It's about immersing yourself in the energy or vibration you hear. If you are able to listen effectively and attentively, you will have the ability to file it away in your memory to recall it later when needed or reproduce the sound.

Scientifically speaking, this transformation is known as "Acoustic absorption."

I can hear a song being sung and immediately memorize the tune. I start singing it back to myself over and over again until I get the melody, rhythm, notes, and hook just right. Most of us can do this if we fall in love with a song.

Music is about memorization and repetition. Almost anyone, except for those who are hearing impaired or tone deaf can hear a good song and replicate every note. We can argue it's not just the song alone that inspires us or make us support a certain entertainer or buy their albums. We are fascinated by the creativity, ingenuity, feeling the song brings, delivery and message behind the song.

Once a masterpiece is written, it can never be duplicated. It can only be licensed, sampled and recorded again. It can be replayed on the radio. It can be sung across the world, but the original work stands.

In the workshops I facilitate, I always start with asking children and young adults what their favorite song is. Many immediately recall their favorite tune and the lyrics that go along. Often, there is a song I've never heard of. So, I respond by saying, "Let's go ahead and pull this song up and listen to it now."

Without fail, many often interrupt me quickly and say, "No, Mrs. Lonna. We can't listen to that song. We have to find the clean version." I am always tickled. I instantly ask the group, "If It's not okay for a woman my age to listen to the lyrics, why is it ok for them?" The answers and excuses I hear leave me quite amused. My favorite is, "Well, we live in the hood and this is what they play so you can't help but listen."

This is always the turning point of our conversation. The words, lyrics, messages, and things we listen to define us, shape our thinking, and create the environment that dictate how we see ourselves and the world around us.

What words, lyrics, messages and ideas about your life have you been listening or failing to listen to?

When I listen intently to a song I feel divinely connected and get lost in it. I get a picture in my mind and internal space inside opens up. The song finds a place inside my heart that never goes away. It lives on forever. Songs I sung as a child begin to resurface decades later just at a time when needed. Immediately I connect that song to a memory from long ago.

Listening is a skill that's so important. If we don't listen, we have nothing to recall. I often tell my daughter, "You have to learn to listen." When I speak to children in my after-school program I share, "Active listening is a skill." Listening is a skill that transfers across industries, generations, genders, and races.

The art of truly listening is getting more and more lost in the digital age, where everyone's shouting and clamoring for a seat at the table without finding out exactly why we're at the table in the first place. A person that learns to listen effectively, can then speak effectively. They can take the data, information or sound being transferred, absorb it and then regurgitate it at the right time and place to execute flawlessly.

If you ever join a Toastmasters, this is one of the things they work on is getting you to acknowledge and listen when you communicate to your own voice and the voice of others. My listening skills are so keen they often scare family and friends. I can recall a conversation from 10 years ago. I can be asleep around others having a conversation and wake up joining the conversation like I never missed a beat.

I used to date a gentleman who'd stop while we were driving along and say, "You're hearing is amazing." This was also a two-edged sword. I always managed to hear conversations some may have not wanted me to hear or withdraw from loud, abrasive situations or people.

I remember one time I was at a banquet. I reconnected with many I hadn't seen in years. An old friend sat next to me. During remarks, she was so loud I excused myself from the room. I couldn't take it!

Another time, I was out with a friend at a Famous Dave's in a Chicago suburb. We were greeted by such a pleasant waitress who brought our drinks and gave us a warm welcome. To my surprise, ten minutes later another boisterous waitress came to our table. After having a 5-minute conversation with her, I finally had to stop and interrupt her. I abruptly said, "You're very loud."

I don't know where it came from. My friend laughed, and we still laugh about it to this day. However, it was even more telling when other waitresses started coming by the table and thanking me. They were saying things like, "Thank you. Someone needed to tell her."

My hearing and listening skills were so highly sensitive, I had to be careful where I lived, the music I listened to and what I took in around me. If not, I would pick up on every little thing, even things I didn't want to.

Listening is critical. What's even more critical than listening is the ability to love and listen to the sound of your own voice.

If you are in the voice recognition phase, you are slowly starting to recognize patterns in your life. You are hearing your own voice but haven't developed the skill and discipline of listening to it to take action. You realize you have a passion or affinity for something but aren't quite sure what path to pursue.

You start to get bored with day to day activities and recognize you need a change. You refuse to remain stuck. You don't need outside confirmation or affirmation.

In voice recognition, there is an acknowledgement that someone is needed to gently guide you to next phase. You look to define your voice in more clarity. You want to turn it up louder and learn how to live in resonance.

You are ready to move from just recognizing your voice to taking action. You are committed to actively listening to your inner voice and living out your unique voiceprint every day. In voice recognition, you need to refine your ability to listen attentively to the direction your voiceprint longs to take you.

In the music world, we call this ***ear training***. Ear training is an exercise that teaches a vocalist or musician how to identify notes, scales, pitches, melody, chords, rhythms, and intervals strictly by hearing or listening repetitively to certain sounds over and over again.

This exercise helps to train the ear to connect certain sounds a score of music or pattern of notes shown on a page. This way, if a student or performer cannot read the music, they can still learn to memorize the sounds that correlate to the notes to recall each when needed later.

In voice recognition, you just need help developing the skill of listening or ear training to apply it to identifying your own inner voiceprint. This will allow you to further recognize and develop the themes, patterns, experiences, gifts and talents that make you unique, so you can start being led by your internal "North Star."

If you are in voice recognition you are already looking for resources to help you refine your message and connect with others of like mind. In this stage we offer our clients a tool called a "Voice Map Canvas." You can visit the resources page at https://www.iamlonna.com/voice-map/ to download a free copy now.

The Voice Map Canvas serves to help identify the themes, sounds, messages that make you who you are. It helps clients begin to recognize patterns to better understand their voiceprint. Once these patterns are defined, outlined and recognized, we use the tool for further work to help shape your story, develop a roadmap, and take step-by-step actions to begin leaving your mark on the world.

We help them align daily habits with your inner voice and voiceprint. We find once a person connects with the resources, supporting voices, strategies, and networks to begin "Living their song," they become unstoppable!

CHAPTER 8

Identify Yourself

Do you remember the Jetsons? It was the cartoon family of the 21st century. As a child, you could take your imagination on the ride of your dreams fantasizing about the future. George Jetson would often come to a door and need to get in. He 'd have to identify himself using his voice in order for the technology to determine whether or not he had authorization to enter. Ultimately, if his voice was identified, he'd get access.

Or what about Inspector Gadget when he was attempting to solve a mystery? During the show, he'd suddenly figure out another piece of the puzzle. He would run outside to his car needing to get to another destination fast. He'd say, "Go Go Gadget mobile!" The car would identify its owners voice. Immediately, the ignition would start. The vehicle would get in gear and he'd be ready for take-off.

What about when you've watched one of your favorite action movies? There is always a treasure needing to be found or bomb hidden away in a vault at the end. The suspense builds. The hero finally makes it to the vault. Anticipation builds when the hero discovers they can't open up the room or detonate the bomb. They find out only the person's voice who's recognized is granted access to go in to turn the bomb off.

All of these examples show us the power of what can happen when we enter the voice identification phase. We tap in powerfully to who we are and begin to maximize our voiceprint.

After searching for your voice and beginning to recognize it, now you enter the stage of truly being able to identify your voiceprint. You communicate it to yourself, but that's where it ends. Like singing in a shower carelessly – you are yet to define your song. This stage sounds like:

- I know my purpose, but how can I use it to help others?
- How will I use my voice to leave a legacy?
- I know what I should be doing but I'm not quite sure how to get started.
- How can I find the resources to help me maximize my potential?
- I know my song, but It's slightly off-key!

A plan without a purpose will perish. A voice without song is never heard. You need help to move on to the next stage.

When I first started my businesses, I started with one goal in mind: To create a tax-exempt organization for single mothers and children of single parent households.

I wanted to purchase property and build housing that allows single mothers to come live for one year. We would teach self-sufficiency skills. Participants would have bandwidth to think about legacy and their children's future. They'd get safe child care, create a business, shadow healthy living, learn proper nutrition, gain financial literacy, plan their estate, and develop a plan for their future.

So many single mothers are doing the best they can to care for their children with such little resources and support. My own mother raised us alone. She was a business owner but always had about three sources of income to sustain us. I remember her running her business full-time working 12 hour shifts as a certified nurse's assistant to give us the best she could.

In 2002, when she had a brain aneurysm and suffered a stroke on both sides of her brain, our family's world was rocked. Our mother had been the visionary, matriarch, stability and strength for my siblings and I. Her prayers, intelligence and wisdom shaped us into the enterprising, resilient, determined women we are today.

My mother purchased land, bought life insurance, and planned for her future before this traumatic event happened. When her brain aneurysm ruptured, none of that mattered. Over the 5 months of her hospitalization everything she worked so hard for began to quickly slip away.

For the next ten years, my sisters and I attempted to balance the financial, medical, emotional and psychological turmoil of it all. We later found out, she had Vascular Dementia. We also learned when she released she'd need seven day a week, 24-hour around the clock care.

This new reality of living, brought much frustration and confusion. More than anything, it brought late night phone calls from nursing facilities, anger with lack of proper care, fear about the future, and ever-changing family dynamics we often couldn't confide to anyone about.

Honestly, I've always loved, respected and looked up to my mother. It wasn't until the brain aneurysm when I found myself a single mother raising a child alone, that I truly understood the loneliness, stress, fear, isolation, and weight that can come from being a single parent.

After becoming a single mother, I didn't have time to think about myself. I didn't have time to create a budget or plan for the future. I didn't have time to do anything - but survive!

Creating this organization seemed to be a worthy cause and became a life goal. With a small three-year-old, I started traveling the country to learn how to build and sustain a successful nonprofit to meet government regulations, maintain its integrity and fulfill its long-term mission.

Between 2008 and 2012, I met other nonprofit leaders from around the globe, learned best practices and reporting guidelines. When I returned to my hometown in Michigan, I pulled up my sleeves full of zeal ready to begin. I started applying for capacity building grants and meeting with small business leaders to help develop a business plan. I noticed a disturbing trend.

Every time I met with someone, they assumed I hadn't done the work needed to understand my industry and magnitude of what I was taking on. I was sorely offended because not only had I done the research, legwork, and time investment required, I'd worked for several large nonprofits, was raised by a single mother, was a single mother and understood my customer quite well.

Time after time, meeting after meeting, they kept trying to talk me out of what I felt I needed to do. They kept saying things like, "Have you thought about this?" "Well, have you considered?" "What are you going to do for a revenue plan?" "Why does it have to be nonprofit?"

Sure, some may argue that these are just questions, but I beg to differ. A single mother working 2 to 3 jobs, raising a child alone taking time to get help to build their dream experiences enough roadblocks and setbacks in life. Questions like these only to left me depleted and frustrated feeling like I'd wasted time. The unwarranted additional questions left me feeling belittled and unheard.

Each representative appeared to be minimizing my passion and purpose. They appeared to be assuming I wasn't equipped. They assumed I hadn't thought it through well enough. If I hadn't been searching, identifying and listening to my own inner compass, I would have given up. I could have easily thrown in the towel to walk away from something desperately needed in the world.

Don't misunderstand me. Every time I was given an assignment to do, I would do it and follow up. After sending information and continuing to show up, many often would stop responding to emails or offer little help at all. The good news is I was in **voice identification**!

In voice identification, you no longer allow accept no or make excuses. You realize the power lies in your hands. You stop waiting for others to open doors for you and start kicking them down!

You understand you have the keys to unlock and open every resource needed and it's within. You stop asking, "Why not?" and start identifying why you should, why you can, and why you will!

This stage is where you decide to move from just having a vision and hear the sound of your voice to actively stepping out and taking action. You take full responsibility owning your voiceprint. You do something about it.

You map out a course. Your values, friends, activities, and words start to align with who you are, and you get laser focused. Now, you look for greater platforms to express your voiceprint to the world and give back. You know you have a song to sing. You look for ways to brand it, monetize it, make an impact and leave your legacy.

You may need an accountability partner, but it can only be someone on the same frequency who's already been where you desire to go. When you arrive at this stage you realize you possess the power to access the room, detonate the bomb, and gain access to the life of your dreams!

CHAPTER 9

Voice Activation

I grew up during the 70s and 80s watching and living through television. Like most children who spend time alone, my sisters and I primarily spent bonding time in front of the screen. One of my favorite television shows was the "Wonder Twins." Do you remember it? It was a brother and sister superhero team.

The show first appeared in Hanna-Barbera's "All-New Super Friends Hour." When the two were faced with taking on a villain they'd join hands and say, "Wonder Twin powers activate!" Immediately they would be endowed with special powers and strength to perform what was needed. Before activating the pair was just two ordinary people who couldn't change a thing. After activation it was an entirely different story.

If you have stopped searching outside yourself, recognize your unique voiceprint, identified what you need to do and have started to take action, "Congratulations!" You've entered into full voice activation.

Everything you do revolves around your purpose and voiceprint. You're totally immersed in your message and are starting to carry your message to the world in everything you do. You're ready.

You have a support system, but don't necessarily need one. Nothing is going to stop you. You're determined to realize your full potential and reach your dreams. You are driven. You are focused. You're productive.

Those in voice activation are 100% committed to your own voiceprint. You're activating it against all odds. You don't need anyone else to affirm you. You keep going with little support knowing there's an endgame in mind. You sleep, eat and breath your voiceprint and it screams to the world in the subtlest of ways.

These game changers write books, promote them, and go on to do much more. This group doesn't just own a business, they grow it. They often employ others leaving the business to pass on as a legacy.

If you are a voice activator you're living for something much greater than yourself.

You don't just "want to be a speaker." You have something to say and something to offer. You value what you bring knowing you can contribute something no one else can or will.

Voice activators know your dreams will come to pass because you consistently make them happen realizing secret victories every day when no one is looking.

You are ready to help activate others. You are moved to unlock the voiceprints of those who may not have the loudest platform or brightest stage. You live by this creed:

"The fight is won or lost far away from witnesses - behind the lines, in the gym, and out there on the road, long before I dance under those lights." - Muhammad Ali

In voice activation, you realize it's not the top of the mountain that earns you bragging rights, it's the work ethic, the dedication, the commitment, and the climb experienced on the way. Is that you?

We've all heard the saying that most overnight successes don't happen overnight. You've spent a lifetime searching, recognizing, identifying your true voiceprint and now you are moving ahead in confidence and consistency.

I work with children frequently and I often recall their tiny little voices after a long weekend when I haven't seen them for a while. I walk into the room and I hear a bunch of cute little voices saying, "Mrs. Lonna, I missed you." "Hi Miss Lonna, how are you?" "Miss Lonna, guess what?" Their tiny voices and faces brighten my day.

There are distinct times when I can recall one person's little voice from the day. One thing about children's voices is that they are very honest and blatant, but also a little shaky and quivery. They are still discovering who they are.

Those small voices transform and mature as they get older. During puberty they go through a time of transition. You'll often hear their voice sometimes crack or deliver a message with a tad bit of uncertainty. I have a 12-year-old and we are experiencing that transition now.

In contrast, adults ages 20 to 30 have strong, confident voices full of promise and ability. Likewise, if you are in voice activation you no longer waiver in what you stand for or believe. You speak and live with boldness. You belt out to proclaim. You're ready to make sound waves and impact the world. Again, I ask, is that you?

CHAPTER 10

Tools

Now that you've identified which stage of the voice-print journey you're in. Here are additional tools to help you project your life into full "voice activation."

The process of unleashing a voiceprint is painful and embarrassing at times. There are parts of ourselves we often want to keep hidden or repressed to avoid associated memories. While writing this book, I struggled with balancing how much to share when recalling things, I 'd forgotten or were in denial about.

Truthfully, some memories had been buried. Recently, I had flashbacks attempted to sort out my own relationship woes. Many suitors perceived me as "a tease", "hard to get", or often referred to me as "Mother Teresa." Frustrated by the dating process, I became a relationship cynic. One day as I pondered why some who pursued me for years, didn't get me at all, it hit me. They didn't understand my voiceprint.

It started to dawn on me I had hidden painful childhood memories and family secrets I hadn't divulged to a soul. Vivid pictures started coming back to mind. I started to remember why I struggled with the duality of embracing my femininity and sexuality while also attempting to do the "right thing" and maintain my reputation as a Christian.

None of it was because I was a "good girl." It wasn't because I was a "virgin" or so "holy." It was simply because I'd never seen intimacy expressed in a healthy way within boundaries. All I had known all my life was extremes. These harsh realities came through introspective self-dialogue.

Facing the truth wasn't easy at all. If you are not 100% committed to finding and unleashing your voiceprint, I encourage you to put down this book and walk away unconvinced and unchanged. Or, if you're like me and can't stomach the thought of living a "humdrum" life without leaving a lasting impact, this is the chapter for you!

I am a very detailed person. Ask my friends. Sometimes, too detailed for those who like things laid out in simplicity. For you, I have created a Voice Map Canvas.

The canvas serves to help provide a roadmap to gain greater awareness of the messages, themes, experiences, and patterns that make you who you are. These discoveries help better understand your unique voiceprint. Once recognized, we can use this tool to unleash our full potential in a more profound way. To download a free copy visit https://www.iamlonna.com/voice-map/

For others, like me who really appreciate the journey of self-discovery and understand knowledge of self is a powerful weapon, I've created the voiceprint Workbook and Guide. This tool includes a copy of the Voice Map Canvas and deeper reflections on the principles shared in this book. Visit https://www.iamlonna.com/shop-now/ to purchase a copy.

When I started writing this book, I shared thoughts with a friend. She said "Lonna these concepts are life changing! I'd love an accompanying journal." So, for those like my friend in Tennessee who appreciate capturing personal thoughts in a more meaningful way, I also offer the Voiceprint Journal. You can purchase a copy by visiting https://www.iamlonna.com/shop-now/.

Now that you know what additional tools and supplements are available at https://www.iamlonna.com/, I'd also let you know the tools that have helped me personally. Many times, so called gurus only tell you enough to keep you coming back with empty promises your life will change if you join their group or purchase the next big product.

I have never been into gimmicks, quick get rich schemes and temporary fixes. I believe change is hard work and an inside job. I'd like to pull back the curtain in my own life and share concepts that really helped transform my life and thinking.

Reading written materials from other voiceprints has been a huge tool along my discovery of my own potential and power. I want to share three of the best books I've ever read. One is the bible. It's simple enough. Learning about God's love, my identity in Him and the fact I was created in His image has given me promise, hope, and purpose.

The other is the Alchemist. I recommend this book to every young entrepreneur I meet. It has so many hidden gems within. I read it in one day. For someone like me who easily gets bored and distracted, that is a miracle. I stopped and wrote down every nugget I found and found every book or resource mentioned within.

I also recommend a Jewish Phenomenon: The 7 keys to the enduring wealth of a people. I buy it for those I love. It contains trajectory shifting principles about raising children, leaving a legacy, and connecting with your roots.

Vision boards have also been a tool to help reinforce my purpose. Previously, I didn't think too much about them. It wasn't until I met Sholanda. She started sharing tools that helped on her journey. I decided to give them a chance. I found the power wasn't in the visual board itself but the process of taking time to think about your future to put action behind it with intentionality and focus.

Affirmations also really changed my life. Some voices in my own head needed to be drowned out with the power of my own voiceprint. When how you are raised conditions you to live below your birthright and potential, you need to consciously plant seeds through your own words daily to influence your thoughts, feelings, and mind. Positive affirmations allow you to hear the sound of your own voice rooting yourself on. You become your biggest cheerleader and loudest chorus.

Next, changing my frequency changed my life. We'll talk about frequencies more in the next two chapters. For now, I will share this. I had to change my associations, mindset, and environment. I couldn't depend on voices of yesterday to carry me where I needed to be. I deliberately and intentionally surrounded myself with opportunities, relationships, and spent time doing things that aligned with my voiceprint.

During this process, I tuned out all the other voices that came to mute me, stifle my song, and strip me of my power. Up until I walked in full voice activation I was naive about people and things. I kept giving people the benefit of the doubt. I made excuses for why things I wanted in life hadn't happened. I kept looking outside for answers from unaffirming voices talking me out of my dreams. I had to tune them out.

Lastly, I began using the principles my ancestors used when sharecropping and began sowing to reap. I started to sow my time into people, activities, projects, and thoughts that aligned with who I was. I discovered if I wanted to reap a harvest and hear the sound of my own voiceprint, I needed to deliberately invest my energy in things that would reflect it.

Every day I started planting seeds to reach my end goal of helping children and parents who lacked strong support systems. I started with what I had no matter how little or small. I spent energy doing and being. This became my primary focus instead of just going to events to fill my calendar and fill a void. I started affirming myself, accepting my voiceprint, and doing me.

As you use the principles and tools found in this book to unleash your highest purpose and potential, send an email. Let us know how you are advancing on your journey. We'd love to hear how your life transforms. Email us at liveyoursong@iamlonna.com. Tell us about how you are moving forward to fully activate your voiceprint within.

CHAPTER 11

Get in Motion

Now you have the tools to start unleashing your voiceprint into full voice activation. Let's look at a few additional laws that govern the universe. If you embrace each, they'll help you get in motion and propel you through the universe to resonate and leave a legacy to impact the world.

I won't go into a deep scientific explanation. I'll just touch on each lightly. Then, we can extract what's needed to become closer to discover and live our unique voiceprint. Two basic laws govern the universe. They are:

1) The law of the speed of light, and,

2) The law of the speed of sound.

We won't go in depth about each law, but here's a brief overview of exactly why these laws are so powerful and should be immediately applied along our journey to unleash our purpose and potential. Before we discuss each, let's first touch on the simple laws of motion.

Newton's Law of motion states "A body continues in its state of constant velocity (which may be zero) unless it's acted upon by an external force." In the principles and thoughts outlined and shared in this book, that "body" is you.

Your life is continuing in a constant moving state. Your life is designed to always move or bend in a certain direction. It will always continue to move in that direction unless it's acted upon by an external force.

Why is this important?

You must understand early on and if not then, now. Unless you set out to define your own life and live life on your own terms, **there'll always be external forces or others acting upon you moving you in a direction you may not want to go**. It may be people, unexpected circumstances, environments, jobs, or other people's greed for power over your life acting upon you to influence you.

Newton's second law of motion states "For an unbalanced force acting on a body, the acceleration produced is proportional to the force impressed; the constant of proportionality is the inertial mass of the body." **Your ability to be successful will depend on the focus and force you put into discovering who you are and staying true to your chosen path.**

Genesis 1:26-28 (King James Version) reads "And God Said, let us make man in our image, after our likeness: and let them have dominion over the fish of the sea, and over the fowl of the air, and over the cattle, and over all the earth, and over every creeping thing that creepeth upon the earth. So, God created man in his own image in the image of God created he him; male and female created he them."

I used to hear this scripture read over and over and wonder what does that mean? What does it mean to be created in the image of God?

Growing up in the church and knowing the bible, a daughter of two preachers, singers, and songwriters, I had absolutely no idea what it meant to be created in the image of God.

I thought it meant if God was good, I was supposed to emulate His persona. I needed to "walk in the light" and "show people His light." I imagined a great big God sitting on His throne full of royalty, high and majestic looking down at the world while everyone bowed at His feet. For me this was overwhelming and humbling.

I attempted over and over again to live up to this great big fairy tale I painted for myself. Imagine my frustration when I failed over and over again. Imagine the devastation when my human nature and frailties kept showing up. How could a person so imperfect be created in the image of an all knowing, all loving, infinite God? Had everything I believed since I was little been a lie?

It wasn't until a few years ago I discovered the meaning to this hidden truth. I hit a real low. I was miserable and very few knew. Stressed and depressed from being a single mother holding down multiple jobs, I was 100-pounds overweight. Years after delivering my daughter I struggled with binge eating and losing it. I finished my 4th degree and wondered "Will this endless cycle end?"

I felt stuck with no way out. I didn't go out the house and was withdrawn from friends and things I loved. I felt I was living a mediocre life where others outside admired my strength and tenacity, but I wasn't being authentic to my own self. I was not "Living My Song."

During this time, I reconnected with a childhood friend who studied Reiki and had made a huge transformation in his life. He too was the son of a preacher. We were on the phone having a very deep, life changing conversation and he said to me, "The reason you're not happy is because you're a creator. Your creativity is dying to come out. You're looking for ways to create."

He said, "You see we are created in the image of God and God is a creator."

The light bulb finally went off in my head and it hit me. "I am created in the image of God." We began to have revelatory conversations about "deliberate creation." I knew that I was on the right path and my own voiceprint became much clearer.

Newton's second law reminds us that unless you "deliberately create" the life you want to live and pursue the things that make you who you to define you, you can potentially set yourself up to be "acted upon" and "impressed" by a force stronger, greater, and louder.

Newton's third law underscores the reason I felt it necessary to write this book. It states, "In a system where no external forces are present, every action force is always opposed by an equal and opposite reaction force."

You may be asking why is she continuing to give us a physics lesson? What does this have to do with me? I am glad you asked.

If you're tired of being stuck and living life the same from day to day this chapter is for you. If you feel as if nothing outside of you motivates or pushes you to change it's for you. If you're torn because everything that currently surrounds your life is competing for your attention forcing you to go in a direction you don't want to go, it's time for you to make a conscious choice to get in motion.

Are there currently external forces or voices that don't match up to the voiceprint you feel inside? Is there a voice saying you can do more, are destined to be more, and there is more for you?

What forces do you currently hear telling you the reasons you can't achieve your dreams? Is it because you're black or white? A Muslim or Christian? A single mother or divorced? An Ex-Felon? A recovering addict?

What voices keep telling you your life will never change? It's time for you take action, find your voiceprint and live it!

Now let's talk about the two laws I mentioned at the beginning of this chapter. We'll look at the laws of ***light and sound***. Why is this so important?

Another law of physics was established by Pierre de Fermat. Fermat's principle states, "the path taken by a ray of light between any two points in a system is always the path that takes the least time." It's imperative to understand why the laws of light and sound must be important to you in pursuit of unleashing your purpose. Let me explain.

As Fermat points out that "the path taken by a ray of light between any two points is always the shortest path. This bears repeating, "**The path taken by a ray of light between any two points is always the shortest path.**

Think about that. If you want to take the best and shortest path to quickly unleash your voiceprint, you must constantly be surrounded by light. Many times, we know what we want to do as little children and somehow between being a child and adulthood, we get deterred from that path. We lose our inner voice and give up on our childhood dreams. ***To ensure you stay in a path of light, always take the path that aligns with your purpose and who you really are.***

Like everyone, I knew exactly what I wanted to be as a child and would tell everyone everywhere I went. They'd ask, "What do you want to be when you grow up?" I would respond, "A star." I knew I was destined to shine, but I didn't know how. I'd see entertainers on tv like Whitney Houston and something would click.

What did I see? I'd hear stories of singers being discovered and think, "Hey, that's supposed to be me." Experience taught me a lesson that I want to avoid many having to be taught. The older I became, the reality of becoming a star seemed less within grasp.

Instead of going after my dreams harder, I looked at other options. Plan A took a backseat to plan B? Other voices louder than my own drowned out the desire to sing, live, discover and invest more in my own voiceprint and dreams.

Having that light or voice in front of you is so critical to making sure you take the shortest path to succeed. This path brings life's greatest joy and greatest sense of purpose. This path allows you to live your best days.

Christians find this light in prayer and the word of God. Others find this light through great parents who lead them on the path t at an early age. Those like my high school classmate Derek Jeter or my friend's son John Legend. Both had parents who saw potential in their children at an early age, pulled it out and encouraged each to have confidence in their path and pursue passion.

Some find that light through friends and mentors like President Barack Obama who became one of the greatest Presidents of our generation and in U.S. History. Fresh out of law school, he was mentored by his would-be wife, Michelle Robinson, also known as First Lady Michelle Obama.

Let's look deeper into the next two laws of the speed of light and the speed of sound. I won't get into a scientific debate or attempt to retest hypotheses and theories. I'm not a scientist. They've been tested. I'll highlight basic concepts.

Light does not need any other energy or outside force to carry it from one place to another. It travels fast and as a wave. It speeds through space in a vacuum at 186,400 (300,000 km) per second. It travels in a straight line. The wave does not grow smaller regardless of how far it travels. It goes in all directions.

For the purpose of this book, we can apply this law to sight or vision. If you have light having discovered your voiceprint, you can get to your destination to unleash it much faster without wasting time getting pulled in other directions. Nothing and no one can distract you or alter your course.

Light or vision is the best path forward and quickest way to get to where you want to be. I encourage you to surround yourself with voiceprints that have vision into your future. Take the time needed to really see yourself, become self-aware, and do the internal work.

Light is so critical to our lives and paths because every major invention, technological advancement, and forward-thinking accomplishment happened because someone caught hold to the revelation of what it means to move through the universe at the speed of light. They make a major discovery using this law to impact everything around them. They change status quo and become a force to be reckoned with. They start to make an impact in the universe. Some even learn to move at "lightspeed."

But what do you do when you don't have light? What happens when you can't see your way? When your lost or confused about your purpose? Consider the child that has lost both parents and has no sense of identity or direction? Or what about the child raised by a single parent who may not have the time to nurture and rear the child where they need to go?

What about the elderly person who has been written off and forgotten who has no mentors or no friends? What do you do when your environment and those around you don't reflect who you really are, what you want to offer the world or what you believe? What do you do when you are dreaming it but can't see it? What do you do when you are absent of light and therefore cannot use this "speed of light" principle in your life?

I 'm glad you asked. Let me let you in on another little scientific nugget you may have overlooked. What is the next best thing to causing changes in the universe if you don't have light. It's **sound**.

Ask the blind man who can't see a thing. He can detect the direction someone is standing, or a car is coming from based on what's heard. If you don't have light in your life and can't use the "speed of light", you have to be able to move with the speed of sound."

This is why you have those raised in certain environments written off to fail, who beat all odds. They tune out the noise and sounds of other voices around them to tap into their own. They are led by their "inner compass" or voiceprint. This voiceprint then leads to the light. They begin using the speed of light and the speed of sound to accomplish anything they desire. They become powerful weapons in the universe no one can reckon with.

If you don't have light or vision, then you "must" have sound!

Let's quickly review the law of the speed of sound. Determining the speed of sound cannot be calculated unless you know certain factors to complete the equation. It depends on the actual medium used to transport sound. Is it being transported in liquid, gas, or a solid. The environment the sound is carried in makes a difference to how fast or "the speed" the sound is delivered.

Next, you have to also review the frequency and length of the sound being transported through the medium. Sound travels through sound waves. You must count the number of waves passing in each second or the frequency. Then, you multiply the answer to the length or wavelength of each to find the speed.

I won't provide numerical calculations but instead dig deeper into this principle as it relates to unleashing our voiceprint. The sound carried and delivered depends on the environment used to carry it, the force behind the sound, and how fast and long the waves are carried when transported.

Each person is able to deliver their message to the world differently depending on the environment they were raised in, how often they are tapped into the sound of their own voiceprint, how long they have been focused on the message and the energy and force invested into unleashing it.

I call this sound voice. If a person can tap into their true voice and begins to transport that into the university they begin to live in the place of voice activation.

As I mentioned earlier voice + vision = velocity.

You must begin to see yourself fully unleashed and walking in purpose. When darkness comes in your life and you can't see, you must begin to listen to the sound and strength of your own inner voice to tap into something greater than you. This is where vision boards and affirmations help.

They provide vision and voice when you can't see it happening or life is overwhelming, and circumstances seem hard. If you can live from this place of focus with vision and voice, you will see speed and velocity happen in your life.

Doors will open that align. Relationships longed for will unexpectedly show up. You begin to produce at a rate you've never seen living your life in "surround sound."

CHAPTER 12

Frequencies

Are you familiar with frequencies, and the impact they have on your atmosphere, environment, mental state, and body? I wasn't introduced to them until about 3 years ago. I was going through a huge personal transformation and a tumultuous time in my life and once again turned to what I had always knew, "good music."

I started searching YouTube for new soaking music to ease my mind at night and find a way to relax. I stumbled upon a video that said "432 HZ" music. I began to read the comments.

Visitor after visitor kept saying the same thing, "listening to the music worked." I listened and was intrigued to learn about what had been called a "healing frequency." I'm a researcher and wanted to learn more. There was a time in history when all music was played in 432 HZ. It was known as the frequency of love.

I began to dig deeper and discovered there were all types of different frequencies." There were lower and higher frequencies. There were frequencies of light, healing, those that provoked change, those that ignited transformation and more.

If you are not familiar with frequencies, there are six main vibrations identified as the Solfeggio Frequencies. They are:

- **396 Hz** – Liberating Guilt and Fear.
- **417 Hz** – Undoing Situations and Facilitating Change.
- **528 Hz** – Transformation and Miracles (DNA Repair)
- **639 Hz** – Connecting/Relationships.
- **741 Hz** – Expression/Solutions.
- **852 Hz** – Returning to Spiritual Order.

If you continue to research frequencies you will learn there are numerous frequencies in the universe and each frequency has its own sound.

By definition, the word frequency means "the rate at which something occurs or is repeated over a particular period of time or in a given sample." It's also defined as, "The rate at which a vibration occurs that constitutes a wave, either in a material (as in sound waves), or in an electromagnetic field (as in radio waves and light), usually measured per second."

In otherwise, a frequency is how sound travels or the rate at which sound travels through the universe. As I studied this more, it dawned on me why as a singer, I was no longer inspired to tune into MTV or my local radio station. I was turned off by present day music because I couldn't relate to the frequency.

I started to recognize that as humans we are truly a product of our environment, what we believe, the choices and frequencies we choose to take in and listen to. If we stay on a higher, positive vibration, our perspectives will be bigger and our outlook brighter. Those on a lower frequency often struggle to find joy in life. Some feel overwhelmed waiting, hoping and praying for the light at the end of the tunnel.

What do you do when your voiceprint is not designed to be motivated? How do you change your frequency?

Sometimes to tune out the noise of our past and silence the negativity around us, we must make a conscious decision to change the direction of our lives by changing our frequency.

Find and connect with others who have voiceprints bigger and louder than your own. In time, you'll learn to listen to it, take it in, get in sync, stay in key, and take your voiceprint to the top of the charts. Remember, you have to be willing to do the work.

Let's explore.

I went through a period where I couldn't stop living in the past. I kept recalling conversations, experiences and friendships examining where they went wrong. I inherited a photographic memory from my father. So, I really took broken promises and relationships that went sour hard.

I'd have conversations with family members about things that happened in the past and they would say something like, "Get over it" or "Let it go." I couldn't let it go. I needed to acknowledge the pain and needed to connect with someone who understood.

I was so intertwined with my family that I felt like I needed them to get me. I wanted them to acknowledge all I'd gone through, affirm me and feel my pain. I was on a certain frequency that hadn't changed for some time.

One day after having a long talk with myself. I realized I was holding on to an idea of what I thought my family should look or be like. I resented the fact I didn't see it in my life. I was attempting to share my experiences to revive relationships of the past, gain greater appreciation and respect. It couldn't happen because I wasn't the same person, and neither were they.

I was still in the process of discovering my voiceprint and they knew me as "Just Lonna." They had no clue the cross or burdens I carried. They didn't truly know me from within. I spent over 20 years away living by myself, building friendships, experiencing life, and venturing out on my own. I expected them to support me, help lick my wounds and nurse me back to health.

It wasn't until I made a choice to let the expectations I had go, move on and choose to support myself in the ways I needed, I became truly free. I stopped needing the approval of those closest to. I surrounded myself with people whose frequencies reflected the sounds and healing I wanted my life to reflect.

My circle grew smaller and my telephone conversations shorter. I stopped being the ear everyone could run to whenever they wanted to dump their thoughts on me without reciprocating.

I changed my frequency. I changed the perspectives around me. I changed the expectations from within. I changed my conversations. Ultimately, my family relationships began to change too. They started to see the parts of my voiceprint I wanted to reflect and acknowledge who I really was.

Changing frequency is more about changing our mindset within. As our mindset changes and shift, so do our behaviors and outer actions. Our relationships change. Our conversations change. Our belief systems evolve.

In my personal life as, single woman there were times I connected to the wrong conversation, partner, or emotional state. I ended up on a frequency I found hard to pull myself out of. I came across men operating on their own frequency who assumed because I was a woman in need of being serviced and rescued, sex was automatically built in to a potential new relationship.

Emotionally, I was torn between compromising what I truly wanted long term for a temporary feeling of companionship. Many potential suitors were not on the same page. They weren't looking for long term commitment. They were still weighing their options and playing the field. I had to make a choice. Do I hold out for what I really want and recognize my own worth or do I stay tuned to this person's frequency?

A glass of wine, the wrong conversation or even just listening to a good love song, could easily trigger this vibration. Connecting to friends living from this frequency didn't help and exacerbated my efforts. It often left me depressed and confused. I wondered if I'd find real. Changing my mindset, desires, network, and friendships to align with higher frequencies is the one thing that helped.

Changing our frequency can be difficult. It's not always easy. Sometimes it's hard. More than anything if we want to fully unleash our voiceprint, live our song and reach our dreams, it's necessary.

Take time to examine the frequencies you've been operating from. Name the top 3 that do allow you to fully unleash your voiceprint. What can you to change them?

1) ____

2) ____

3) ____

CHAPTER 13

Echoes and Riffs

In my own life, there are several times I felt muzzled and muted. Some are painfully too hard to talk about. Many know about my journey to realize my lifelong dream of become a globally recognized recording artist. I've shared this earlier. What I don't often talk about is the shame that stifled me when I found myself a single mother raising my daughter alone and 100 pounds heavier than when I started.

I hid from the world. I stopped singing. I couldn't possibly take to the stage. I was so concerned about my weight and appearance I stopped interacting with family and friends. I was depressed and muted. Looking back, it's interesting because I honestly hadn't gained as much weight, but over time I obsessed about it so much I gained more and more.

This was a hard time. It was a strong support system, friends who accepted me as I was, and those voiceprints I heard cheering me on kept me going. I'd like to share more about a few special people.

My mother is a huge part of my voiceprint. Her resilience, tenacity, hopefulness, encouragement, and pursuit of excellence is interwoven in my DNA. I carry her song, love, and inspiration with me everywhere I go. Many always remember her beautiful smile. I can honestly say I never saw her cry or flinch in the face of opposition.

My father influenced me greatly. The late Reverend Eugene Hardin passed in March of 2017. I never grew up with my father, but we grew close the last 20 years of his life. Even now I miss him and always have. I learned the most about his voiceprint from other people but understanding more gave me glimpses into my own identity.

I will forever treasure his compassion for people, wit, charm, loyalty, dedication, family values, service, political activism, and intelligence. He had a photographic memory. This often is a part of my voiceprint that I'd love to exchange. I often hold on to people, memories, events, and information long after they've moved on.

My sisters Brenda, Margi, Vanessa, and Renata definitely inspire and give purpose to my voiceprint. They were the first to recognize my laughter, extroversion, and love for the spotlight at an early age. We often suffered many things together that we couldn't tell a soul. I love them dearly for I see my mother and father's s smile, warmth, brilliance, and delicacy in each of them. We had hopes of changing the world and we each are in our own unique way.

There are voiceprints who impact us not related to us that are still like family. Clara Grayson was one. She was an amazing woman who I met in 1992. Classy, graceful, and full of fire, she always stood for what she believed.

Originally, from Alabama she raised 7 children, loved God, and made everything beautiful she touched. Her hourlong telephone conversations, prayers, and homemade zucchini bread was just what a young girl needed to see the value in gleaning from her wisdom and love. She passed of cervical cancer in 2003.

It took me years to grieve. She is still such a huge part of my voiceprint. I often pray one day she'll look down from heaven and smile knowing her deposits weren't in vain.

True friends are hard to find. I have a lot of friends, but just because you're a friend to someone doesn't mean they are a friend to you. A friend sticks closer than a brother. A friend loves at all times. I can definitely count my friends on two hands which is more than some.

I personally want to thank each of my dear friends who have served as voiceprints during some of my lowest times. They each accepted me as is. Some embraced me when I had nothing to offer but a silly smile or innocent naivety. Navea Harris, LaTonya Stewart, and Audrianna Redding helped me through some hard times. Each of their beautiful voiceprints contributed to who I am today.

Faith and spirituality have always been a part of my voiceprint. Both of my parents were preachers and gave themselves over to a life of service. Growing up in church, I encountered many prayer warriors and soldiers that added to the sound of my voiceprint. My first pastor and his wife, Elder Willie and Marion Mitchell, were definitely that.

Baptized at the age of 7, I found a love and appreciation for the word of God and giving back to my community. Years later, my voiceprint was also strengthened by Pastor Ricky and Tria Hunt during my teen years. I explored my love for choir directing, leadership, and singing as a member of their congregation.

Bishop Hugh D. and Pastor Letha Smith of Embassy Covenant Church International were who I looked to during my formative adult years. The pearls of wisdom and revelation I learned while serving under their tutelage at Emmanuel Covenant Church International is priceless.

I'll forever hear Bishop words as a spiritual mentor echoing in my ear. His words of correction were often unwelcomed and unheeded, but even now as I persevere through many hardships and successes, his words planted in my heart continue to produce a harvest.

Many point out they can name their friends on five fingers to point out the scarcity of finding true friends. I can honestly say I've been blessed with several friends and an unwavering support system through some of tough times.

That said, there are friends who truly stand the test of time and stick with you whether with crowds or in a valley alone. Ronald Stephens, a.k.a. "Pop Legend" is one of those friends. Our unusual introduction is something we often still recall.

It was 1999, I finished my first solo recording as an independent artist entitled, "Praise Him." I wasn't well known in those days except for the Pentecostal Assemblies of the World where I traveled during conventions performing at midnight concerts when given the opportunity.

At age 25, after attending more conventions than I want to admit, I found myself bored of redundant preachers wandering from vendor table to table looking for something to give meaning to attending yet another event. To my surprise, I ran into a bright, friendly, and warm personality who appeared much more ambitious and gifted than I.

This was quite unusual and even more unique was the fact he was at 20 years older but so down to earth. "Pop Legend" or Ronald Stephens could hold a conversation with anyone, but his artwork, charm, kindness, and genuineness was even more inviting. He asked, "What do you do?"

I responded, "I sing." He challenged me immediately on the spot, "Sing something." I did. The rest of the story and our friendship is history. We became great friends. Artist to artist he encouraged me to pursue my dreams and talents. He himself was an author and artist and sowed his own work into me inspiring me to do more.

From that day, he was always the friend that brought me back to my true voiceprint and challenged me to keep reaching for the stars. Ironically, when I found myself pregnant as a single mother, it was him who drove two hours to make sure I knew all would be well. Our 15-year friendship produced a love for God, hope for the future, and loyalty that friendship is not based on temporary circumstances but in believing always in each other, "the best is yet to come."

It was Ron's faith and my own witness into his personal success journey that encouraged me to keep pursuing my highest hopes and seeking to be the best woman I could.

Years later, I was privileged to see his own story unfold as his son John Legend continued to break records in the music industry, defy odds, unleash his voiceprint and leave his mark on the world.

It was this inspiration that kept me going through the hard times and kept me believing that the impossible and unimaginable is always within reach.

Looking back, there have been so many that have inspired me and allowed me to echo their victories, triumphs, successes and follow in their path. Darlene Morris is one of those people. I met her in my early 20s after joining Emmanuel Temple in Battle Creek, Michigan. On fire, full of passion and zeal, I volunteered and signed up to be a part of anything that made me believe I could bring transformation and change. I had just rededicated my life to the Lord.

Looking back now I realize this is not a once in a lifetime decision we adamantly make and proclaim, but instead a life of constant reflection, daily sacrifice and the need to make this decision over and over again.

Giving my life back to God is where I received and still receive initial training and preparation for marriage. Times I hated the woman I'd become. I wanted to walk away and leave to start anew. Suddenly being reminded what drew me to God in the first place and how the thought of Him and His voiceprint revive me over and over again.

Running back to His love and back to His arms to ask for his forgiveness, acceptance and embrace during my lowest times. He's so consistent, so precious, so faithful, so humble, so silent at times when we need to grow the most and a huge part of my voiceprint.

I met Darlene Morris during one of these times. As I mentioned, I volunteered for an initiative the church was undergoing. It was a 24-hour prayer chain where we petitioned God about our new church edifice and the next step for our ministry. I took the night watch with prayer hours between about 12:30 or 1:00 a.m. I had no clue what I was doing and had never done anything so self-sacrificing. I thought it was amazing and wanted to contribute my voiceprint.

The person leading the prayer before my designated time would need to call to hand the baton off. I was a new member and so had no clue who anyone was. I remember the morning like it was yesterday. I was awakened by a phone call. I answered with sleep still in my voice, "Hello." The voice on the other end was calm and reassuring.

She said something to the effect of, "I am passing this on to you." Then she continued, "While I was praying the Lord said to tell you, "You carry the song of the Lord. It's a song of healing and deliverance. It will bring you before Kings and take you places you've always wanted to go."

There was more but I take off guard. You see when I gave my life back to God in my early 20s I walked away from my passion and desire to sing. I pursued a recording contract most of my life believing I'd be a star. I knew the messes and contradictions that pursuit had gotten me in to.

I have so many horror stories of finding myself stranded in

cities believing some industry executive who said he would pay fare home, if only I'd get there. Or what about the time I met the strange man who proclaimed to preach the gospel who later attempted to kidnap and hold me hostage in Highland Park, Michigan?

I was even homeless for a brief stint at the age of 19. I was so careless, so reckless, so blind to what I wanted I was willing to do anything to reach my goal.

So, to hear this loving, warm, and confident voice on the end telling me I "carried the song of the Lord" was mind blowing. How in the world would and could God entrust His song with someone like me? Not to mention a song of healing and deliverance, but wait, "I needed to be healed. I was just getting delivered from so much, so many childhood scars and memories." Really?

It was just too much to take in and too much to ponder at 1:00 am. Nevertheless, I appreciated being on God's mind and Him thinking about me. I took the experience and conversation in and then forgot every single word she said by the morning.

I was devastated. I'm like... "Wait! What did she say?" I honestly didn't even think about it or look back, but when I showed up to church the next Sunday, guess who approached me? Darlene. Not only did I get to meet her face-to-face, but she brought the exact words she spoke to me typed out on the most beautiful paper and framed! That day... my life was changed. I had new purpose, new meaning to my voiceprint and I felt inspired to dream, be, and do again.

Later, she would become one of my greatest life mentors. She would talk to me about things I never knew or understood. She would spend hours on the phone pouring her wisdom, love and direction into me. When I received my first internship at the Kellogg Foundation while still getting my undergraduate degree, she would take me under her wings and show me the ropes. When I needed a job after my internship ended, she started teaching me Executive Administrative Assistant skills while I volunteered in her office at the Battle Creek YMCA.

Even greater, when my mother suffered her brain aneurysm and stroke and I could no longer feel her strength, wisdom, counsel and advice near, it was Darlene's voiceprint that stepped in to fill the void. It was a huge one to fill and after I found myself pregnant as a single mother it was her healing, reassuring voiceprint that loved me back to life, supported me, became my daughter's Godmother and kept encouraging me through a difficult time.

She brought diapers when I needed them, bought my daughter coats and clothes when I had nothing to give in return, braided my daughter's hair when I was clueless what to do with a newborn little girl. For every one of my hurdles, defeats, victories, family struggles, and daughter's birthdays she was there. I am not sure I would have made it to the place of maturity to write this book without her. Her life is not just one of my echoes... but one of my riffs. It's the kind of riff that when others hear it, they wonder... "How in the world did you do that? Darlene Morris and all the others like her... that's how?

It's the power of a voiceprint.

There are so many other amazing people who assisted along my journey of introspection and helping to fully unleash my purpose. Ethel Fitzpatrick, a dear friend who is an amazing wife and mother continues to be one of my biggest cheerleaders. She taught what it means to be a wife who sometimes has to lay low in the cut to support the greater good. Every Southern Bell I've ever known has been an amazing cook with an unusual grace to make a happy home. She inspires me in the subtlest of ways.

Lastly, Sholanda Cox, a dear friend and confidant, I was fortunate to meet in 2014 during my time working from home for Uber. We started in rider support while the $120 billion-dollar company was still in its infancy and only in 6 markets. We were each promoted numerous times. The company quickly grew scaling to bring more riders and partners on the platform. We offered our wisdom, skills and strengths long before Uber branched out to UberBlack, UberEats, UberBoat, and many more ventures.

Sholanda and I started on the same team but were quickly dispersed to other departments throughout the company. She transitioned to Driver Support Tier 2 while I transferred to Uber Everywhere. The new team which would help the company grow from six markets to more than 354.

After transferring, I thought I would never hear from Sholanda again. She was so sweet and quiet. In team meetings, she rarely said a word. She worked long hours, but outside of our roles that was all I knew.

One day, I logged into HipChat our internal chat messaging tool and found a private message from Sholanda waiting. When I went to read it, my life was changed. It said: "Lonna please like TinyKidney.org, the Facebook page I started for my daughter."

I clicked on the link and was floored to find out who the person behind my computer screen was. The link connected to a Facebook page with a picture of the sweetest little face. Samaya Cox was in need of a kidney and her mother had started an organization to raise awareness and gain support to help.

My silent, sweet coworker was actually so much more than I ever imagined. I was challenged and inspired. In my mind I had been thinking I was burning both ends of the stick. I worked long hours as a single mother working two jobs to make sure my daughter had a better life. I felt alone and as if no one understood my struggle.

Only to later find out this woman was raising her children alone, homeschooling them, running a few businesses to bring in multiple income streams, working with me, running a Facebook page and caring for a child with special needs. I was completely caught by surprise and humbled.

I realized at that moment that no matter how tough we think we have it, someone somewhere is going through much more. Sholanda and I became best friends. We became more like sisters. I learned from her and our relationship stretched me. She began motivating me, giving me advice and ways to make "Melody's Song and the City of the Voice Snatchers" a reality.

We would spend hours on the phone talking about our visions, businesses, and dreams for our children and how we would make it happen. She believed in the power of my voiceprint and I believed in hers. Her voiceprint was exactly what I needed at that time in my life to push me to do just a little bit more, complain a lot less, and keep believing that what I wanted was within reach.

Samaya finally received her kidney. The kidney transplant brought new struggles, new conversations, and new prayers. I received my first completed book project which brought new hope, new responsibilities, and new opportunities. We both remain the best of friends and encourage each other. We often say we need more friends like us in our lives because... everyone needs someone to unveil their true voiceprint within.

We all need someone to expose our pain. We don't need those who just celebrate with us on the mountain. We need those who almost saw us die in valley. They come down to cry and wallow with us. Then, with the little strength they have left, they lean down to pick us up to carry us up the hill to drink from a quiet stream.

Many in my own journey who contributed to the power of my voiceprint are unknown faces and names who would never tell a soul about the amazing traits they hold or awesome things they've done. We don't always have to shine so bright that the crowds come. Sometimes it's that candle or flashlight in the darkness that allows someone to survive through the night until life's wires get fixed, the electricity is working again, and the lights come back on which is much more potent and powerful.

To every voiceprint that has us inspired us to do more, be better, and live our highest dreams, "Thank you."

ACTION STEPS

Make a list of the top 5 people in your life who has contributed to your voiceprint.

How do the times you shared with them make you feel? What inspires you most about them? What are the ways they inspire you to be better and do more?

1) ______________________________

2) ______________________________

3) ______________________________

4) ______________________________

5) ______________________________

CHAPTER 14

Time to Break the Sound Barrier!

Now, it's your time to choose. How will show up? Voice actor, voiceover, or voiceprint?

Will you take a leap of faith to go after your dreams? Will you tune out the voices of negativity telling you they're not within reach?

Will you show up with an active or passive voiceprint?

If you chose to live from your authentic voiceprint and answered yes, it sounds like you're in the perfect position. You are ready to break the sound barrier!

"The sonic barrier or sound barrier is the sudden increase in aerodynamic drag and other undesirable effects experienced by an aircraft or other object when it approaches the speed of sound. The sound barrier was originally broken in the 1940s.

A sound barrier is broken when the conditions line up and are just right. The aircraft's wings, the area rule, engine and performance all determine the outcome.

We've provided the principles and tools to help. We've equipped you with the lift, thrust, and outline you need to get in motion. The rest is up to you. The power lies in your voice-print and in your hands.

When you fully embrace your voiceprint, your life will take flight. Conditions will be just right to break the sound barrier in your life. Things holding you hostage to your past will have no choice but to let go!

Once this happens you will began to create sound waves. Next, those sound waves will generate shock waves. This is where your sound begins to travel faster than the speed of sound. When this happens, your life or voiceprint begins to produce a huge amount of sound energy and then guess what?

Sonic boom! Your sound. life or voiceprint will start to create as it moves through the universe breaking barriers, defying status quo, and beating odds.

Your voiceprint will then take on a new sound and create an explosion that has to be recognized, listened to, and taken in.

We've seen lives transformed through our group coaching sessions, consulting, and training sessions. In those settings we share our framework and dig deeper into the concepts shared in this book.

We know true happiness comes in being able to, "Live Your Song," not someone else's. Give yourself permission to unleash your passion, purpose, power and project. Someone's waiting on you. Your sonic boom or explosion is the sound others are waiting on to step out, step up, and step in to their true calling or voiceprint.

Don't wait another day. Start now!

Made in the USA
Monee, IL
13 September 2026

62979540R00083